TODDLER DISCIPLINE

A Helpful Guide with Valuable Tips to Nurture Your Child's Developing Mind

SIMON GRANT

© Copyright 2020 - All rights reserved.

This document is geared towards providing exact and reliable information in regards to the topic and issue covered. The publication is sold with the idea that the publisher is not required to render accounting, officially permitted, or otherwise, qualified services. If advice is necessary, legal or professional, a practiced individual in the profession should be ordered.

From a Declaration of Principles which was accepted and approved equally by a Committee of the American Bar Association and a Committee of Publishers and Associations.

In no way is it legal to reproduce, duplicate, or transmit any part of this document in either electronic means or in printed format. Recording of this publication is strictly prohibited and any storage of this document is not allowed unless with written permission from the publisher. All rights reserved.

The information provided herein is stated to be truthful and consistent, in that any liability, in terms of inattention or otherwise, by any usage or abuse of any policies, processes, or directions contained within is the solitary and utter responsibility of the recipient reader. Under no circumstances will any legal responsibility or blame be held against the publisher for any reparation, damages, or monetary loss due to the information herein, either directly or indirectly.

Respective authors own all copyrights not held by the publisher.

The information herein is offered for informational purposes solely, and is universal as so. The presentation of the information is without contract or any type of guarantee assurance.

The trademarks that are used are without any consent, and the publication of the trademark is without permission or backing by the trademark owner. All trademarks and brands within this book are for clarifying purposes only and are owned by the owners themselves, not affiliated with this document.

Table of Contents

Introduction 1

Chapter One: Your Growing Toddler 6
    The Emerging Toddler Personality 7
    Easygoing and Relaxed Toddlers 8
    Highly Active Toddlers 9
    Parenting Suggestions for Highly Active Toddlers................... 10
    Highly Sensitive Toddlers... 13
    Parenting Suggestions for Highly Sensitive Toddlers 15
    Cautious and Slow to Warm Up Toddlers 17
    Parenting Tips for Cautious Toddlers 19
    Highly Intense and Inflexible Toddlers 20
    Parenting Suggestions for Highly Intense and Inflexible Toddlers 23

Chapter Two: Emotional and Mental Development 25
    The Toddler Mindset 26
    Toddler Emotions and Brain Wiring 27
    Feeling and Thinking.. 30
    Emotions in Children 32
    Girls, Boys, and Emotions 33

Learning How to Express Feelings 35

Toddler Emotions 38

Chapter Three: Why Toddlers Push Limits 40

Why Toddlers Push Limits 41

Chapter Four: How to Talk to Toddlers 48

Communicating with Your Toddler 48

Chapter Five: The Toddler's Need for Boundaries 53

Chapter Six: Ditch the Distractions 60

The Problem with Distraction 61

Better Than Distraction 64

Chapter Seven: Why Toddlers Suck at Following Directions 67

Why Your Little Rascal Rebels 67

Chapter Eight: The Art of Staying Unruffled 73

How to Rock the Art of Cool 74

Chapter Nine: The Toddler's New Baby Blues 81

Dealing with Adjusting Toddlers 83

Chapter Ten: The Truth about Consequences 90

What Makes Consequences Fail 90

Beneficial Consequences 93

When Parents Disagree 97

Conclusion 102

References 115

Introduction

Welcome to the most amazing adventure of a lifetime. The one adventure that beats Jumanji: raising a child. They start as babies, grow to become toddlers, then adolescents, teens, and one day, you're looking at a full-grown adult.

A toddler is a little somebody that can walk just fine on his or her own two feet. I guess you could say they "toddle" about. "Toddler" is a word coined from two Scottish words, "todder," and "waddle." It basically describes the way babies stand up and try to walk around, sort of like a drunken sailor with legs shoulder-width apart and their arms outstretched or above their head. There's a lot of lurching around involved, too.

I suspect that you will soon experience the most amazing aspects of life with your toddler. He will intrigue you with his passion for world exploration, clever shenanigans, endless spurts of energy, the spontaneous nature of his affection, and how he expresses it.

Leaving the constraints of babyhood, he transitions into the world of an independent child. His knowledge of boundaries and even self-starts to take place, and when this happens, your little bundle of joy will be less joyful than you'd like. He will begin to throw tantrums. He might stiffen, and even point-blank refuse to be strapped into the car seat or stroller. She might refuse the food given to her. She might get very upset at your inability to read her mind. Something as simple as refusing to let her exchange toys with her friends or playmates are major triggers for baby tantrums. These behaviors are very typical during this unique and incredible stage of human life.

Toddlers are more prone to push and test your limits than you think. It is how their brains are wired, seeing as they are active explorers and equally active learners. Besides, developmentally, this is appropriate behavior for their age. These outbursts and less than appreciated behavior are a natural expression of the whirlwind of emotions jumbled up inside them as their struggle for autonomy continues.

Proper and adequate guidance ensures the children's comfort and safety while they flourish. When the boundaries you have set as a parent are functional, you'll find that the little ones don't test them often. They tend to be very trusting of their parents or guardians, and with these boundaries in place, they definitely feel more relaxed and freer to direct attention to the things they consider important, like learning, playing, socializing, and just living as happy-go-lucky children in general.

As a parent or guardian, when setting up boundaries, you'll notice that your current emotional state is sure to almost always reflect in the reaction of your child or ward. So, if you lack confidence and transparency, or in other words, you lose your cool, seem tense, frustrated, unsure, or even frazzled, you are likely to unsettle your toddler, and that could lead to even more unpleasant behavior.

Imagine you are a god in the eyes of your child, and your emotions always dictate the tone. With this knowledge, it is pretty easy to understand why toddler discipline and its struggles can quickly become a less than pleasing ordeal. In my opinion, no kid is bad, per se. They are just conflicted and very impressionable. They are battling with impulses and new emotions while trying to express their needs and feelings the only ways they are capable of. Each time you think of them as bad when they frustrate, offend, or confuse you, you are doing them more harm than good, because being called a bad person is like having a negative stamp on your back. This source of humiliation can eat so deeply into their psyche that they might even start believing it. My idea of parenting and my perception of the relationships we have with the little ones are all from trials and errors.

When it comes to your little ones, there are some important things you should take note of. For one thing, babies are aware, communicative, sentient, and intuitive. They are quick learners, natural explorers, and scientists, in the sense that they test hypotheses, figure out ways to solve problems and make successful attempts to understand abstract information and languages. This might not be what you would call parenting wisdom, but scientific findings and clinical research have confirmed these facts about children. That said, if you're like most parents, I am willing to bet that you still treat your little angel as if she is unaware, incapable of effective communication, and vacant. This very incorrect logic can lead to a lot of guardians and parents in a very counterproductive direction with regards to toddler discipline.

Ultimately, the secret ingredient to proper child discipline is throwing all the gimmicks, manipulative tricks, and quick-fix tactics in the trash and actually being really honest with the little ones, as I will explain in this book. This is the simplest form of respect.

You see, your toddler should develop language skills at about 12 months of age. These skills will take a huge leap from two or three words to a gigantic vocabulary of about a thousand words or more at the end of two or three years. During this time, your toddler will learn to make short, but intelligible sentences that make total sense. His physical skills also take a huge leap at this point, because he goes from barely standing by himself and taking some wobbly steps to more concrete movements like climbing, running, kicking, and jumping. Other skills in his life will take major leaps as well. You get a once in a lifetime chance to show your toddler the world. You get to have wonderful adventures together, while you discover yourselves and each other on this beautiful journey.

You wonder why I say you'll discover yourself? Your child will teach you so many things about yourself. You get to experience the luxury of walking slower than usual, so you can watch the caterpillar try to climb a tree; the spontaneity of making random shapes with damp sand and then punching through them so you all can start all over again; and you even get to splash in mud puddles, just because. Children get to have all the fun, don't they?

The fact of the matter is that there is a lot that we could still stand to learn when it comes to parenting. You may have often had the feeling like you not have a single clue what you're doing when it comes to raising your kids. Or, perhaps you would like to have kids, but have held off for a while because you're not quite sure what the best approach is when it comes to disciplining your toddlers. It could very well be that you never really had a good relationship with your own parents, and as such, you would rather spare yourself the heartache of bringing kids into the world only for you to get it wrong with them. Well, you don't have to worry about that anymore. With this book, you will learn that there really is no one size fits all approach when it comes to training your toddlers so that they can grow up to be the best versions of themselves. No one really ever gets it perfect, but at least once you read this book, you will definitely have a much clearer idea of how to take care of your kids, and how to discipline them. You don't have to worry about whether or not you're going to be too lenient or too harsh anymore. Simply follow the guidance offered in this book, and you will find yourself falling in love with the process of caring for your little ones!

This book is a guide on toddler behavior and the ways that respectful parenting can help shape a toddler's life for the better. It will definitely be a great benefit to you and your child. We will be looking at common toddler tantrums, cooperation, setting boundaries, punishment, and much more. Let's begin.

Chapter One

Your Growing Toddler

Every parent can surely agree that every child is different. In fact, most parents go as far as to say that their own child is unique — which isn't a far cry from the truth. Think of it this way: The same way each person has their very own, one of a kind, fingerprint, is the same way each and every child has their unique personality, vulnerabilities, and gifts.

Honestly, the one-size-fits-all theory of parenting definitely does not apply to toddler management, which is exactly why parents are a vital aspect of a child's development. Parents are the best judges of what might be best for their own child. They make this deduction using certain factors like their kid's personality, reactions to events, and level of maturity.

As a parent, one thing you can be sure of is that you will always be in the process of learning because as your child grows bigger and older, you will find clarity in certain areas of her life. Answers to questions you've been quietly asking will slowly begin to unfold. Questions like, "What is my baby most curious about?" "Does she prefer to watch cartoons or play with dolls?" "What would he rather spend time doing?" "What are his vulnerabilities?" "What about her strengths?" "How would she rather learn?" "What has changed about him, and what hasn't?" "How would she rather communicate?"

In this chapter, we'll go over how toddler personalities take shape. I will also offer some guidelines on how to deal with certain unique traits of your child. As I said earlier, the one-size-fits-all idea does not work on children, so pick what you want from the guidelines and leave the rest.

The Emerging Toddler Personality

Temperament is the level of emotional intensity or excitability of a person. Temperaments can be detected in the first weeks after birth. A toddler's temperament plays a huge role in how she reacts to situations and learns from her environment. Sometimes, temperaments can be hard to recognize, seeing how unpredictable toddlers can get. Despite their volatility, temperaments remain unchanged day to day. For example:

- Would you call your toddler a live wire?
- Do you think he's clingy?
- Would you call her easygoing?
- Is he big on exploring?
- Do you think he's shy?
- Is she the kind to take in her surroundings first before making a choice on what to do or where to go?

Ironically, competent parents are usually stuck with very troublesome children, while the not-so-competent ones sometimes get the well-balanced, easygoing children. If you already have kids, you can attest to the fact that wide personality differences are very frequently found among children born of and raised by the same parents. An unpredictable child is very likely to experience irregular sleeping patterns. A careful and delicate toddler will tend to pull back.

Another thing you will definitely discover about toddlers if you haven't already is that they are often acting out this very minute and then mellow the next. Something every parent should know is that being the parent of a toddler does not mean that you have to shoulder the burden of responsibility for behaviors that you have little or no control over. Some traits are even likely to stay a part of the toddler throughout childhood and sometimes well into adulthood. A toddler slows to warm up might turn out to be an adult that is slow to warm up. This applies to other traits like sensitivity, positivity or negativity, and so on. Now, we will be taking a look at detailed examples of typical traits exhibited by toddlers, as well as suggestions for how to deal with them.

Easygoing and Relaxed Toddlers
First things first, we'll take a look at the basic traits of a relaxed and fairly easy-going toddler. Generally, this kind of toddler is described as a good girl or a good boy. All toddlers are good kids in their own unique ways, but these super compliant kids are usually full of positivity and have a cheerful outlook on life. They can't be

described as hyper or sluggish whenever they are up for the day, because they are generally a very peaceful lot, and they seem to have quite a lot of fun even with their moderate activity levels, be it stacking blocks or rolling around on the carpet or taking toys out of a box only to put them back in. Even something as simple as scribbling color on a notebook brings immense joy to these ones. Easygoing toddlers have attention spans that enable them to stay focused on whatever they are doing without straying for too long due to other distractions. This kind of toddler does get distracted — but not as much as others since she has enough focus to engage in an activity for a considerable amount of time. This toddler is very okay with learning to adapt to new environments and situations with very little fuss if any. They also maintain the delicate balance between curiosity and mindfulness. This quality is such a blessing, especially as toddlers are very unpredictable by nature.

Highly Active Toddlers

Highly active toddlers live off the high that is deep muscle sensations. These sensations can be gotten from whirling, jumping off and onto things, climbing, and so on. Toddlers of this nature are attracted to spontaneous and wild activities. They are even likely to go the extra mile to discover new physical activities to engage themselves in. These very strong, investigative urges leave them open to falls and injuries. They might also be prone to restlessness, have short tempers, and prove rather difficult to control. Children like that are not the most patient. They're less likely to wait in a queue, or wait in the doctor's office, or wait for anything, really.

They find toys only as interesting as the meal they had that morning, and even then, the meal probably held their interest longer. The urge to get up and move around or switch to the next activity hits them like a train, and they're on the go. Confinement and boredom are two things that wouldn't be associated with children like these if they had a say on the matter. Being confined to a particular space or rule can lead to aggression, lasting tantrums, or destructive activity. Attempting to strap these little power boxes into a car seat or even a highchair can prove to be a major struggle that might require a few sips of your preferred energy drink first. A trip to the grocery store with high active toddlers can morph into a nightmare, and fast, because they are likely to complain very loudly, play hide seek in the store, jump off the shopping cart and run off, throw cans off the shelves, and do other very frustrating things as they come to mind. In truth, some parents actually fear that their super active toddler might have ADHD (Attention Deficit Hyperactivity Disorder), but at the toddler stage, it is just too soon to tell for sure. The good thing is a lot of highly active toddlers calm down naturally as they get older and gain better control over their physical abilities. They learn constructive ways to channel all that energy.

Parenting Suggestions for Highly Active Toddlers
If you're the proud parent of an overactive one, you're also a very vigilant parent because your kid is more likely to take certain risks than other children her age. Because of this, you're always on the

lookout, always alert, waiting for her next move so you can save her from impending danger if you have to.

It is completely normal to worry about your sanity even while worrying about your kid's safety, so let him have ample opportunity to let out all that physical energy and schedule in breaks for yourself every now and then. If your kid is in this category, I have a few suggestions that you can try for everybody's sake:

1. Exhaust him. Your child needs to be worn out at the end of the day if you are going to get any rest. He needs quite a lot of intense exercise every single day to help him expend that energy. Let your toddler play outdoors. A toddler-safe playground is your best bet because it allows him to get the full outdoor experience without harming himself, hopefully. I say hopefully because kids like this always have ideas in their heads that you would never have thought of. Letting your toddler play outside will also enable him to gain better coordination. You could sign him up for toddler gym class. You could also let him run around as much as he wants in a spacious mall, not filled with people. This should give him all the physical stimulation he needs.

2. Keep her hands occupied. If it is important that your toddler stays still for a few minutes, occupy her hands. Give her something to play around with, like a ball of kiddie's dough, maybe. You can also give her stickers to peel off her shirt or her arms, or a plush toy to roll in her lap, or a colorful magazine or

board book. You can let her toss foam balls if you can be certain that she won't knock anything to the ground.

3. Build a no-accident zone in your house. When having a child, childproofing is a given. A no-accident zone goes a little deeper than that. Creating a no-accident zone means designating a portion of your house to your toddler. This portion is going to be for toddlers only, and it will be built to be a super safe environment for whatever your toddler would like to do. Here, she can move around with no need for your eagle eyes on her all the time. People who do this pick the basement for this, but you know your house better than I do, so you decide. Set up safe contraptions for her to jump around if she wants to. A portable sliding board for kids would also be nice. You could even add a toddler-sized crawl through the tunnel for extra fun.

4. Schedule in breaks for yourself: Anyone who says they can cope with an overactive toddler 24/7 is either another overactive toddler or someone on a juice I don't think I'd like to be drinking. As a parent, you need some time off to recharge, or you might shut down from exhaustion. It is easier than you're currently thinking. All you need to do is find someone trustworthy to take the toddler off your hands at least once a week for however long you need to cool off. You need to take care of yourself if you're going to be fit to take care of a child — and an overactive one at that. If you can find parents going through the same thing, you all can share ideas.

Highly Sensitive Toddlers

Highly sensitive toddlers are like the Pisces of the toddler community. They feel more deeply than most children their age, and it is usually difficult for them to make sense of sensations. Certain sensations like sights, music, lights, temperatures, and sound changes can be a major source of distress to the little ones. Something most people do not know is that not all sensitive toddlers are sensitive in the same way. Some toddlers who are sensitive to touch may find even the softest caress unsettling. A light pat on the head is very likely to result in a violent response like one's associated with pain. Sometimes, they might find their clothes too tight or too itchy. They are likely to get upset by a simple clothing tag. To the best of my knowledge, that seam in every sock is very distracting or annoying to them. Toddlers like these are usually terrified of routine well-baby exams. They might cling to you in utter terror, or have an intense breakdown, which usually precedes a glazed-eyed retreat as if they just went through a major emotional shock.

Apart from sensitivity to touch, there is also sensitivity to sounds or auditory sensitivity. Toddlers in this category are hyper-aware of even the littlest sounds. They might find the soft humming of a fridge to be unnerving. What you might consider a background noise might be completely unbearable to then. Toddlers like this never fully understand the necessity of some every day sounds like barking dogs, doors that squeak, a ticking clock, children playing noisily, the hum of a vacuum cleaner, loud music, smoke alarms, or alarms in general, among the bajillion and one other noise they hear each day. They honestly don't get it, and they might make a fuss about it. So, paying attention as a parent is important.

Another kind of sensitivity is sensitivity to taste. Toddlers in this category are sometimes picky eaters. Flavor, temperature, texture, and other food qualities that hardly bother other toddlers, or even adults can evoke a strong response from these little ones. By "strong response," I don't mean that simple gesture of turning up the nose. Sometimes, the food might be too crunchy, too cold, too smooth, too hot, or too something, and unlike our favorite girl Goldilocks, the toddler may need a few more than three meal options until he finds something he thinks is just perfect. He may even withdraw and try to hide behind you or try some other trick to protect himself from feeling overloaded by sensations he cannot stand.

A good number of sensitive children go into distress or hyperactivity when it's time for bed because their highly sensitive nature makes it difficult for them just to shut down and go to bed. Toddlers like this usually require some kind of nighttime ritual like being wrapped snugly in a blanket or being rocked in a rhythmic fashion until they finally drift off, or maybe being read a bedtime story. If your child has a blanket that is well-used and has a familiar scent on it, it might help her fall asleep immediately or relax enough for sleep to kick in slowly. A teddy bear could work, too.

Highly sensitive toddlers are not very good at group childcare arrangements. They're not the most adaptable. Environments like that can seem overwhelming to him because children are just messy, noisy, and extremely demanding in general. A toddler with skin sensitivity is likely to flinch back at having wet or filthy hands touching him, and this can make him disengage from or refuse to participate in activities like playing barefoot on the grass, or building shapes with wet sand. These are activities that children usually engage in for pleasure. If you happen to notice any of the aforementioned characteristics in your toddler, it could be his way of shielding himself from the wave of stimulation that leaves him in distress and threatened.

Parenting Suggestions for Highly Sensitive Toddlers

I have compiled a list of suggestions for dealing with a hypersensitive toddler. These are merely suggestions, so take what you think will work for your child and nothing more. Let's take a look:

1. You don't have to force it. Attempts at coercing your toddler into being a lot less reactive or sensitive won't do you any favors, because he literally cannot be anything other than his original, hard-to-decipher self. If you try forcing him to act otherwise, you might end up with an even more self-protective and withdrawn child. Your coercion can also lead to aggressive outbursts, and we don't want that, do we? Instead of coercion, try to keep him engaged with activities that relax and calm him. You should also pay attention to his needs and responses.

2. Arrange for security. No, I don't mean bodyguards and bouncers. Something as simple as getting him wrapped up snugly in a bracket can be more useful than you realize. Keeping him around familiar objects help in relaxing him into his environment, and keeps him from feeling overwhelmed by the outside world. Some toddlers get calmed by any kind of vibration, and these days, grocery stores sell battery-operated or handheld vibration devices to help with childcare.

3. Create a nest. Convert a space in your home to serve as a place of refuge for your over-sensitive toddler. It will be the one place he can call his safe haven besides your bedroom, of course. It can be a kid-sized tent or a fridge box with a portion cut out for the door. Place decorations inside the tent or box to give it a homey feel. For decorations, you can use his stuffed toys and plush carpets. This will be the place he retreats to when he is feeling overwhelmed by noise or other children. If you can live in a much more serene environment so that he can focus on listening to a few things at a time and not be deluged by a lot of auditory sensations such as the neighbor's constantly barking dog.

4. Try out other touching options. A few toddlers with skin hypersensitivity prefer deep touches to light ones. Others would rather be gently brushed with a soft-bristled brush when needed. Try gentle requests to play with soft kiddie's dough or clay. This can help the toddler become a bit more comfortable with the idea of having messy or gooey hands seeing as this is likely to

come up in classrooms where she won't be under your supervision anymore.

5. Food creativity works. This is for toddlers who are picky eaters. Toddlers who are frustrated by food textures should be gently introduced to pureed foods. Alternatively, you could let her used her hands to select food pieces so that she can get a feel of them herself before putting them in her mouth. When feeding her, use a soft spoon so that she doesn't mentally create a connection between gum discomfort and eating. Also, you can try giving her a tiny pure fruit pop a few minutes before each meal to see if it will help numb her overactive taste buds so that she will not be overwhelmed when eating.

6. Visual and auditory soothers are a miracle. You should try soothers. Visual soothers work by projecting a particular or a bunch of images unto the ceiling or wherever you direct them to. These images work to relax your child and help her feel safe when it is time for bed. Some examples are fish tanks, nightlights, lava lamps, and much more. Auditory soothers are also relaxants. Examples are calming new age sounds, white noise, rain sounds, orchestral music, ocean sounds, and much more

Cautious and Slow to Warm Up Toddlers

Toddlers in this category are clearly shy, clingy sometimes, and uncharacteristically quiet all or most of the time. Kids like this usually seem worried, sad, or serious, and they often have a pouty expression on their faces.

This toddler is very likely to withdraw when he feels pressured to meet new people or engage in new activities in new environments. Kids recoil at unfamiliar surroundings and situations, but cautious kids do this more than usual. They are also likely to become really clingy and feel the need to stay very close to a parent or guardian.

If you have one of such children, you'll soon find that making forceful attempts to get him to warm up to people or be sociable will only get you nowhere. Think of when you take your toddler to childcare because you have to run a few errands, and you just can't have her tag along. You know those initial protests when you drop her off? Those are expected with every child, but when dealing with a cautious toddler, expect a little more than a few protests. She might even stay sad or angry at you for longer than usual, even if she is in the care of a familiar person like a neighbor or nanny or even a relative.

It is clear that cautious toddlers consistently react despite the identity of the person involved. This tells us that it is not the regular anxiety associated with strangers. Instead of giving a more obvious reaction like the hyperactive toddler would do if stressed or frustrated, this toddler would rather suffer in silence, might retreat, and even become more fearful. To any other person, he might look okay and stress-free, but scientific research has shown that during stress and anxiety, the heart rate and blood pressure of cautious children tend to go up. The cautious toddler is more likely to flourish in a calmer home environment, where he only has to deal with very few children, or in a school for special needs with teachers trained to understand and relate with the little ones.

Parenting Tips for Cautious Toddlers

Up next, we'll be looking at a list of suggestions for dealing with a cautious toddler. These are merely suggestions like I have mentioned before, so take all of this with a pinch of salt. Here goes:

1. Incorporate warm-up time. You should give your toddler enough time to get comfortable in new environments or situations before pulling away. When you do pull away, don't forget to explain that it is only temporary, and you will be back soon. Use kind words and gestures.

2. Do your best not to hover. It is very hard not to want to protect your child from the stress and anxiety that comes with unfamiliar situations, but it will help him more than you think if you give him a bit of space and allow him to be his own person, rather than jump to protect him every time you think he is in distress.

3. When teaching social skills, do so slowly. Teach your toddler to socialize step by step. Start with the simple social skills, giving a few rewards in between while he inches nearer to the mark. Teach him to reach out to others, but do so at his present comfort level. I'll give an example: Instead of forcing your

toddler to say greetings like "hello" and "bye," teach him just to wave instead. He can do this even while keeping his eyes averted to avoid eye contact. When he does this, reward him for being a polite child, and then work your way up from there.

4. Try to set up experiences. To help your toddler build confidence in social settings, try setting up low-key experiences. Something a little private. You can arrange a playdate with a slightly older child, or a non-aggressive toddler at your home, where he will be most comfortable. If he seems to be enjoying himself, stay close by so that he will not be thrown into a state of panic by the thought of being left alone with an unfamiliar face. Don't hover, but stay close. If that does not work, maybe you should come to terms with the fact that your toddler is just fine in his own company.

5. Look out for subtle stress signals. Cautious toddlers or extremely shy toddlers with way too many fears are likely to feel strong emotions like anger but suffer in silence because of the difficulty they have with communication. Do your best to be on the lookout for the tiny hints of stress coming from him. Give him reassurance every now and then with positive, encouraging verbal feedback and hugs.

Highly Intense and Inflexible Toddlers

We can all agree that a strong sense of independence, determination, and solid opinions, despite being seen as important qualities of an adult, can make for a very frustrating toddler.

Toddlers with clear cut opinions are, most often than not, the most challenging kind of the toddler community. "Strong-willed" is usually the term used to describe the children in this category. To others, she might be perceived as ill-tempered or spoiled because her reaction is usually moody or even negative.

So many toddlers exhibit these characteristics right around their second or third birthdays, so the key is differentiating between the highly intense toddlers and the typically stubborn ones. To do this, you need to take notes of the intensity and frequency of your child's stubborn behavior. Usually, toddlers are quick to bounce back and go about their usual exploration or play some minutes or even seconds after feeling upset, but these intense toddlers' kind of settle there for a while. In fact, they go from one upset to another. Throwing baby tantrums once or twice in a few days is understandable, but four or five every single day is a whole different story.

Another characteristic of intense toddlers is their resistance to instructions or rules. A less intense child might throw tantrums over less favorable rules, but will eventually come to terms with it if you hold out a little bit longer. An intense toddler, however, will react aggressively for long periods of time to criticism from others. If he gets a whiff of something as another person's idea or he feels coerced to do something, it is expected that he will stand his ground in defiance.

Daily routine patterns like sleeping and eating are usually odd and irregular. Preparing this toddler for simple things like childcare in the morning or getting him to come into the house after a long time of playing outdoors can be a pain. Generally, transitions are a major hurdle for this child. Behavioral patterns are almost unpredictable. The same applies to his emotions. This means like he is likely to react in a physically aggressive way when you least expect it.

This toddler could also get quite manipulative. For example, she might vehemently choose not to wear certain clothes, and may even react to simple acts of touch as if it hurts her when it really doesn't. She may strongly insist on eating only a few select foods because others might be "wet" or "gooey. "After a while, parents or guardians of an intense toddler soon realize how ineffective all the reassurance, explanations, nurture, reasons, ignoring, punishments, and rewards have been, because these things are not only tiring, they just do not work with these kids.

Unfamiliar situations or environments can make this toddler very anxious, with bouts of stormy anger not far behind. Sometimes, their emotions and behavior get spontaneous, and things get intense, fast. Temper tantrums usually often happen — more than twice a day— and last for 20 to 30 minutes or more. These tantrums include but are not limited to, thrashing around and screaming. This behavior can continue well into his school years and even way past the age when he should have outgrown them.

Public tantrums have to be the worst because people might judge the situation too soon without any knowledge of what is going on. As a parent, you might be classified as a wimp for not setting clear boundaries or disciplining your toddler when you should have. Some onlookers might just conclude that you have raised a spoiled child. Public tantrums are the absolute worst.

Parenting Suggestions for Highly Intense and Inflexible Toddlers

Now, we'll be looking at a list of suggestions for dealing with an intense and inflexible toddler. Again, these are only suggestions. There is no rule stating you have to follow them to the letter. Let's begin:

1. Master the art of staying cool. Despite what most people say, this is a much-needed skill when dealing with an inflexible child. If you react to their tantrums in an inflexible and angry manner, know that you just raise the chances of a meltdown. You might have just dropped a lit match onto a line of gasoline, and if you don't put the fire out as soon as you can, things will definitely go boom between you and your child. If you're trying to react post-meltdown, you need to remember to stay calm. Don't overreact or overdo anything. Remain as calm as you can be.

2. Troubleshoot. Another thing you can do is try to figure out the things that have high chances of setting your toddler off. Isolate those situations that have never failed to cause a tantrum.

Basically, make a note of as many triggers as you can figure out, and then be on the lookout for red flags or warning signs of an impending trigger and act as soon as you notice them. This might not be perfect, but this will surely reduce the tantrums by a lot. No cause, no effect.

3. Avoid dishing out punishments for noise. Punishing an intense child for being loud when she is unhappy or upset is counterproductive. You definitely wouldn't punish her when the cause of her noise is something happy, right? She is a toddler. You should let her be one.

4. As much as you can, don't play the blame game. Whatever you do, try not to take the behavior of an intense toddler personally. You need to acknowledge your efforts and how hard you're trying. Resist giving into the idea that you're a poor parent or a wimp because you do not want to take the blame for situations you can't control. Your child is intense, and you are doing the best you can.

5. Hold fast to a steady routine. Do your best to keep the child's routines as predictable as possible. You can get a little booklet for that purpose only. Scribble down drawings of at least one element of each activity in the routine and arrange them in the order that they will occur. You can go through the drawings with your toddler to prepare her for each transition.

Chapter Two

Emotional and Mental Development

I'm sure you've thought about the reason why your toddler's emotions swing back and forth like a pendulum on steroids. You've wondered how it is possible for your calm, easygoing ray of sunshine to go from all that brightness in one minute to stormy tantrums in the next minute. Positive this minute and upset the next. Going from zero to a hundred really quick.

If you have a toddler, you've probably had those moments where you get an overload of affection that is usually succeeded by baby tantrums and quick fits of rage. A toddler's emotions are not the easiest to predict. While your toddler goes through emotional maturity, she will actively work on putting her feelings into words. She will also begin to realize the presence of emotions just like hers in others, too. This process, however necessary, is a long one. It usually takes a long time for your child to become fully aware of her emotions, and express them as clearly as she can.

On the way to the stage that is toddlerhood, your child begins to develop empathy for others. With enough practice, direction, and encouragement, he will slowly learn how to deal with very strong emotions and channel them in a more constructive direction, instead of the usual destructive approach he used to take. A lot of people never learn this skill even in adulthood, and this is the cause of so many avoidable problems. In this chapter, we will be taking a look into the toddler community, because it gives us big people a clue as to how things really work. As a parent, you should do your best to discover the things that make your toddler tick, and use this to your advantage when shaping him to become a disciplined child. Find ways to encourage his awareness, his ability to get back up after life, shoves him down, and his ability to communicate clearly.

The Toddler Mindset

In order to fully grasp the reason for the importance of emotions during this stage of child development, we'll start from the basic engine that powers the toddler's thought processes: The child's brain.

The way the brain works, in general, helps explain why the little ones get so excitable, resistant, perplexing, changeable, and downright moody. The mind and heart of the toddler grow as quickly as her body. She marvels at the world before her. I mean, she has been around for a few years, but now she truly sees. Her mind is absorbing everything around her: so many sights, so many sounds, so many places to go to.

As she moves on from babyhood, the toddler begins to find independence from her mother. She begins to understand her feelings, wants, needs, and ideas, separate from that of her parents. This new understanding is quite heady. She feels unlimited, but she is, unfortunately. In so many ways. She would very much like to dress, but she can't seem to figure out how the buttons work yet. She just found out that balloons and candy exist, but you won't let her have any or as much as she would like. She knows daddy sat on a particular chair yesterday, but now grandpa is on that exact chair, and she wonders why grandpa is on daddy's chair. So she cries, gets mad, howls, and falls apart, until something distracting enough takes her out of that emotional space.

Toddlers haven't learned to control their desires, bodily functions, impulses, and temper. This new found independence has quite a few downsides as well. Despite her excitement about her newfound self-awareness, the thought of being truly independent is a bit unsettling for the toddler because she has turned to you for food, comfort, sleep, and entertainment her entire life. As such, you can expect this transition to be a bit shaky. Even as she finds her feet, your toddler has the need to reconnect with you as often as possible for reassurance, because you are like a safe haven from which she can explore the world.

Toddler Emotions and Brain Wiring

In the brain, you have synapses. These synapses are nerve connections that receive information conveyed across the brain through the help of certain chemicals called neurotransmitters. The switchboard of a toddler is so complex that one brain cell is capable of connecting with a lot of other cells — maybe even fifteen thousand cells. By the time he clocks three years old, his brain would have created about a thousand trillion connections, which is roughly twice that of an adult's. As he moves into his teen years, his brain will begin to do a lot of disconnects. It will start to cut off a lot of unnecessary connections and start to form a more organized pathway of nerves and neurons. When he reaches adulthood, all the other negligible side directions and potential pathways that his brain could have followed would be completely nonexistent. All gone. Poof!

A toddler's brain works round the clock. It can be compared to a living electrical loom. It goes on weaving new ideas all through the day in order to form a map of who he is, how he fits into this vast world, and what he wants for himself. I'll give you a quick breakdown of what happens to our brains from the start to adulthood. Roughly around the 8th week of gestation, the brain is responsible for all the major processes that are required for survival, like the heartbeat, body reflexes, and breathing, among others. Then, it proceeds to link the many other parts that are required for the body to run, like the brain's emotional centers. At this time, your baby is creating about 250,000 new brain cells every minute.

Moving on to his first year after birth, the weight of his brain doubles due to it becoming a little more complex than before. Think of it as an electrical organ switchboard. When he gets to his mittens, the brain begins to make connections between the portions of the executive cortex that is located in front of the brain. It does this in preparation for the next phase of life, adulthood. The major function of the executive cortex is to oversee higher thought processes like the ability to think abstractly, concentrate, make decisions, withhold emotional impulses, and find solutions to complex problems.

During toddlerhood, the capacity of the brain to perform those higher mental processes is very low because the parts of the brain responsible for said processes haven't developed yet. However, the areas of the brain in charge of emotion are very active, despite not being fully developed. This gives a bit of insight as to why your child is quite impulsive, repetitive, and uninhibited. Her forgetfulness, newfound self-awareness, meltdowns, frustrations, and feelings of others are all part of the development of her brain. The same applies to her inability to word her feelings. Oddly enough, during old age, as we inch towards the end of life, the brain somewhat rewires itself and then degenerates. This is responsible for the childlike behavior exhibited by elders.

The truth is that your toddler isn't stubborn on purpose, or spoiled, or just plain frustrating. His developing brain still has a lot of work to do. Your toddler might behave in fits and become unpredictable at times. This is because all parts of his brain don't develop together. Some are currently developing, while others are just giving them a head start. A typical full-scale meltdown, however brief, occurs at times when his brain is being overstimulated or becomes challenged. Don't worry, because, with time, all this will pass. In about 36 months, you'll be waking up to a much calmer and amenable child.

Feeling and Thinking

While going through the toddler stage, the two most important tasks your toddler must accomplish are, first of all, experiencing feelings, then learning how to link actions to emotions and how to word them. Scientific studies have revealed a link between toddlers' comprehension of feelings and emotions and their language skills. Apparently, the quicker they understand language, the quicker they understand emotions and feelings. These things take a lot of time and practice.

The emotional facility can be likened to learning how to go up and down the stairs or being able to speak a full, intelligible sentence. Quite a number of toddlers actually begin to describe their feelings with words as early as 20 months. A good example of the words used by most toddlers to describe their feelings is "happy," "sad," "okay," and so on. When they reached about 24 months, most of the toddlers who participated in a study could use at least one word to express how they felt — words like "mad," "sad," etc. — but they couldn't exactly differentiate the two expressions on a person's face yet. A few months later, they became able to make two-word sentences like "Mommy sad," "I 'fraid," and so on. The results of this research have been echoed by many other similar studies.

There comes a time in every toddler's life, where her feelings and her understanding of how she feels exceeds her expression and language skills. Basically, her emotions are too complicated for her to express at the time. This period usually takes place when the child's brain is busy trying to get its network in order to prepare for higher mental processes. Since your toddler can't really use words, other extremely frustrating means of expression come into play like biting, screaming, and tantrums. When your toddler clocks about 20 to 30 months of age, her verbal expression skills start to peak, really quickly, and at right about the same time, the emotional storms and tantrums will begin to lessen, and she will be much calmer than before.

Toddlers with slow language development are an exception to this, as are a few others. When your toddler finally reaches his third birthday, he will be much calmer than he was in the previous year and a half. Your toddler will find it much easier to express himself in more detail now. He will also be able to talk about the most recent feelings he remembers. He will be able to use "feeling words" like happy or sad when classifying other people's emotions. He is still unable to grasp the meaning of so many other emotions, like how a person can feel more than one emotion at the same time, but that is okay. His little brain will get there soon enough.

When toddlers reach the end of toddlerhood, a few children become capable of combining their newfound feeling words to make simple sentences, and this shows that they acknowledge the existence of another person's feelings. They might even come up with new feeling-word combos. However, until your toddler's communication skills skyrocket and she's able to tell you how she feels, she is going to get very frustrated sometimes, more so because, for some reason, a lot of toddlers somehow expect their parents or guardians to understand how they feel despite their inability to spell it out.

As she matures and her ability to understand and explain what is going on with her matures as well, expect your child to resort to gestures, wails, tantrums, facial expressions, and body language in order to pass her message across. Wait it out. It won't last forever.

Emotions in Children

The ability of a child to deal with his own feelings has a lot to do with him being brought up in a world of affection, warmth, and acceptance. When a child is emotionally supported during his early years, it will show in his self-esteem, his connectedness with you, and how he interacts with people — including his life partner — all through his life.

During the highly emotional stage of toddlerhood, he will likely get his most basic knowledge about emotions from you, his parents, or guardians. Knowing that you are his first emotion coach, you should understand that he is learning all he can about feelings from the things you say and the way you express your own feelings to others around you — especially the people you care about. He is paying rapt attention. Some parents are most talented in the art of teaching emotions, while others are not as good, for a number of reasons. They might still be in getting the hang of it all, themselves. This is not a terrible thing. After all, you can't be a great teacher at what you do not know, can you?

Leading by example, you will begin to demonstrate the emotions that are acceptable from your toddler to them. You also teach them about emotions that, if expressed, could land them in trouble. If you're likely to yell and scream whenever you get upset or frustrated, if you tend to express yourself physically, then your child will most likely mirror these lessons he learned from you while interacting with others. At this stage, your toddler's main focus is higher-level abilities like how to delay gratification, read body language, and take cues when given. Your toddler right now is learning how to control his impulses and how to feel empathy. He is pretty much trying to use his thoughts and understanding of his emotions to manage the bumpy road that is called life.

Girls, Boys, and Emotions

It has been noticed that a lot of parents are really influenced by gender when it comes to how, where, and when they express emotions. Studies have shown that some parents express emotions differently when dealing with a male toddler than a female toddler. They show a larger range of emotions for the females and much less for the males, which is why girls are generally better at expressing their emotions than boys. A study that made parents observe and interpret a child's emotion discovered that when the parents were told to observe a female child — despite the actual gender of said child being male — they usually interpreted the emotion like fear, but when they were told to observe a male child — despite the actual gender of the baby being female — they usually interpreted the emotion as anger.

Another research done discovered that a lot of parents frowned at angry girls but smiled at angry boys. Some parents — mostly fathers — have been noted to give a positive response to a male toddler's irritability and a negative one to the exact emotion in a female toddler. This usually has to do with the parents' belief that certain temperamental characteristics and emotions are strictly for boys, while others are for girls. This leads to a lot of parents to react solely based on gender.

Further studies have shown that male toddlers expect a negative response or reaction to their expressions of sadness, and this makes them express that particular emotionless. The female toddlers expect a negative reaction from their mothers to their expressions of anger, but a positive reaction or response to their expressions of sadness, so they tend to express more sadness and less anger than male toddlers.

During the process of regulating emotions in toddlerhood, the art of regulation doesn't necessarily equal the elimination of emotions or changing them from one form to another. What it truly means is that they learn to control the intensity of their emotions. Think of it as learning to work the volume button on the TV remote. It is important for your child to learn to regulate his feelings so that they are less and more intense when necessary. This control will ensure that he doesn't get swept up by strong emotions.

Toddlers are not equally gifted in the art of emotion regulation. Some are more gifted than others. A child who is shy may feel sadness and anger as intensely as a hyperactive child, but will not be equipped with the confidence to express said feelings properly. What he is likely to do is retreat or lash out at others, while he desperately tries to stay afloat in a sea of emotions that threaten to drown him.

Toddlers are very gifted at manipulating the length of time they feel emotion for. Over time, they also get skilled at managing emotional changes. For example, a toddler might mute his excitement when he walks into a birthday party to give off an air of sadness. He does this so that he can get all the nurture, attention, and cuddles he needs at that time. He does this because time after time, he has learned that this is the absolute best way to get the attention he wants, or whatever else it is that he's looking to get out of acting that way at that time. I'm sure you don't have to think too long or too hard to realize a few times when your own toddler has pulled this pretty frustrating trick on you so that she could get whatever she wanted, be it a chocolate bar, or a cookie. It's funny how we know what's going on, but we fall for it more often than not anyway.

Learning How to Express Feelings

Learning to maintain the delicate balance between feelings and how to express them is a skill that will require your toddler to invest lots of time and dedicated practice. As I have mentioned before, some toddlers get the hang of it much sooner and even better than others, but this shouldn't be a yardstick to determine their character or personality when they become adults.

If you have a toddler already, you must have noticed that one emotionally charged word that holds special meaning to the toddler is "no." During the toddler stage, this word can mean quite a lot of things. It is possibly her way of reminding herself not to do certain things, or it could mean that she is trying to tell you when something she needs is missing. "No water!" Yet another popular way your toddler uses the word no is to get away from a person she doesn't like. Sometimes, it could mean her trying to inform a person not to take away something she's currently playing with or holding on to.

There are a few ways to assist your toddler in self-expression. We'll be taking a look at five possible methods for effective toddler communication:

1. Signing. While your toddler is still trying to get the hang of verbal communication, you can try to teach him to use sign language to express his feelings. This may go a long way in helping him communicate, and could ultimately reduce the frustration that comes with the inability to let you know what he thinks and feels. There are very simple signs to express certain feelings, as opposed to bottling them up and eventually lashing out. You can teach your toddler to use the sad face or wipe an imaginary tear from their eye when they feel sad. For anger, he can put on a scowling face or make a fist. For happiness, an index finger on each side of a big grin on his face should do the trick. Practicing these gestures with your toddler is so much fun and strengthens the bond between you two. There are quite a few other ways to teach your toddler how to sign. There are videos online, as well as articles and even websites such as

www.signingtime.com. You could always come up with something new on your own, too. You know your child best!

2. Reading. Teaching your toddler to read boundless advantages. There are certain picture books that provide visual information on what emotions are all about. "How Are You Peeling?" by Saxton Freyman is a kiddie's book that contains large pictures of fruits and vegetables which show various emotions. "The Feelings" by Todd Parr is another kiddie's book that employs the use of stick figures of animals and people to represent different emotions with a touch of comedy. "Carrots or Peas?" By Anthony Lewis is another one that lets toddlers determine the emotion of the child or children on each page. "My Many-Colored Days" by Dr. Seuss is a simple kiddie's book about the basic knowledge of everyday feelings.

3. Looking at images. Gather a few pictures of children, adults, and even babies showing different feelings. Put them all in a scrapbook or photo album. The pictures can be cut-outs from old magazines or downloaded and printed. Place the photo album within reach of your toddler in case they would like to take a look when you're not around. Take some time to go through the pictures with him and explain the different emotions. You can also get a mirror so you can both try to copy those expressions. Look into the mirror and use the word and facial expression to convey an emotion, then he can do the same.

4. Putting Words to Feelings. Your toddler should be free to express all kinds of emotions as long as she does nothing to hurt someone or damage property. If she can't exactly put whatever she is feeling into words, you should help out by saying the words for her. She is likely to repeat after you or nod her head. Good examples include, "You are really upset about this" or "You are happy I'm home." Another route you could take is to ask her how she feels. You could say, "Can you say 'mad'?" or "How do you feel about this?" This will encourage her to make more attempts at putting her feelings into words.

5. Taking cues from others. Toddlers learn by watching and mimicking those around them. They will be encouraged to express their feelings when they watch you do the same. Kids pick up things really quickly, so it is good to drop the right crumbs. They will pick up expressions like fed up, bored, impatient, excited, confused, tired, proud, comfortable, tense, relieved, nervous, and scared. When they hear these words, you're unconsciously laying the foundations for your toddler's emerging vocabulary and awareness of the complexities of human feelings.

Toddler Emotions

This is a quick guide to assist you in reading your toddler's emotions.

- **Pause.** The first thing to do is slow down. Take a moment to pick up your toddler's cues and try to discern them. This will give you an insight into what he may be feeling.

- **Make a decision.** Once you have figured out what you think or know your toddler is feeling, the next logical thing is to figure out if the time is right for a lecture on emotions. If it isn't, maybe later.

- **Validate your discovery.** Get to eye level with your child and emphatically tell your toddler what you think she is feeling. While you do this, keep making observations, until you find that one statement that results in a look of recognition on your toddler's face. That's the jackpot. Now you are completely sure about her feelings.

- **Solve the problem.** The solution to the problem can be a variety of things, depending on what the problem is. You could choose to take action, or maybe set boundaries if necessary, while you explore alternatives with your toddler. For example, if the child is sad because he would like to go home, you could choose to say, "We can't leave right now, but you can play with my keys if you like." Or, you could choose to say, "Do you want us to leave now? We can if you'd like."

Chapter Three

Why Toddlers Push Limits

The act of pushing limits can confuse even the most attentive parent or guardian. I mean, why would your little angel throw her teddy at you right after you told her not to? As if that wasn't enough, she would smirk for effect. Is she plain evil, or does she feel a growing need to practice her throwing skills? Does she hate you or something? I'm happy to tell you that it is none of those things.

Toddlers who have high sensitivity, feel intensely and are terribly lacking in impulse control sometimes use fewer pleasing ways to get their messages across. If it makes you feel any better, these toddlers don't even fully understand these behaviors themselves. The real explanation behind these behaviors is the combination of developing prefrontal cortex, and the volatile emotions that are a major characteristic of toddlerhood. In simpler terms, toddlers are easily engulfed by impulses or emotions that are too complicated for their immature brains.

In truth, your toddler probably heard you loud and clear when you said you didn't want her hitting you, her siblings, her pets, or her friends. She completely understood when you instructed her not to spill water or food on the floor or scream and say cuss words, but being the toddler, she is, her impulses chose to do otherwise. She may even smirk after obviously defying you, but this isn't out of spite like it may seem.

The first rule to note when dealing with toddlers is never ever to take it personally when they test your limits. Our babies love, are thankful for and depend on us more than they can actually express yet, and you need to repeat this in your head until it has its own billboard in your head.

A healthy perspective and deep understanding of limit-pushing behavior are very important. Understanding and acknowledging a toddler's stage of development and not reacting violently to their behavior is a crucial aspect of respecting him. Most of his behavior is completely age-appropriate, and even if he has to be disciplined, it must be done the correct way. Abuse is not discipline. Let's take a quick look at a list of reasons why toddlers push limits.

Why Toddlers Push Limits
Stress from hunger, fatigue, or boredom. For some reason, toddlers are usually the last people in the world to realize their own hunger or fatigue. They might be hungry or exhausted, but they just keep playing or doing whatever it is toddlers do until it gets dire, and they have to resort to limit-pushing behavior to get some attention. It's like their body just decides to take matters into its own hands because the toddler clearly can't get the message.

Each time I'm asked about toddler limit-pushing behaviors, the first thing that comes to mind is exhaustion. There was a time I was babysitting but had to rush to a store that was having a fire sale that day. It was all nice and smooth. He seemed fascinated by all the clothes and all the colors until he suddenly started pushing and kicking. I automatically knew that he was exhausted and had had enough of all that. I informed him immediately that I heard him and that we would be out of there soon. I told him, "Stop kicking. You're tired, aren't you? Ready to go, yeah?" Unfortunately, I got tangled in a conversation with someone I know right there in the store, and it slipped my mind that my nephew wanted to go home. Unsurprisingly, he kicked again. That one was on me. I told him, "Sorry, love. I know I said we'd be leaving, then I got caught up in a conversation. Thank you for snapping me back. We're leaving right now." He probably didn't understand half of what I said, but he understood the emotion behind my words.

Another good example is a family trip; we had some summers back. My son, who was four years old at the time, said a cuss word to my mother. That was very uncharacteristic of him. Most parents would start to worry about where he picked that up, but I wasn't. Toddlers hear things. They learn. They are more attentive than you think. What I was worried about instead was why he did that. What was the reason? With the determination to stay calm, I told him, "You cannot speak that way to grandma. We're leaving right now." I took a screaming toddler out of the room. I was upset, but I didn't let that influence my actions. I took him to another room where we could both calm down privately, and then it hit me: We were on the road for about five or six hours. He must be exhausted, and that was the only way he could let me know. That was on me.

What I'm basically trying to say is that you should not assume the worst when your child does something out of character or something that would make your grandma blush and look at you with disappointment. Make sure it's not a matter of just hunger or something like that, and you and your toddler will be just fine.

Seeking clarity. Another reason toddlers push limits is that they're seeking clarity. They're trying to draw a straight answer from you. They're trying to understand exactly what you meant when you set a particular limit, and this is simply one of the ways they do that, as opposed to simply asking. Being toddlers, their communication skills aren't exactly topnotch yet. They push limits to get answers to the many questions running through their little heads like, "What happens if you're tired? Can I do it then? Will you let me try on Tuesday evening when mommy is back? What if you're a bit cranky?"

By pushing limits, the toddlers are pretty much doing what they're supposed to do, which is educating themselves on our leadership, getting a much clearer understanding of our expectations, having solid knowledge on house rules, and understanding power dynamics in the household. Toddlers very much like to know where they stand in the scheme of things. The one thing we can do is to give a direct answer as calmly as we can. The variation of our responses is a given, but they should always demonstrate that we are totally unfazed by their limit-pushing, and we can deal with it.

Understanding the fuss. As a parent or guardian, each time you lose your cool, give an unreasonably long lecture, direct a little too much or even speak too much on limit-pushing behavior, you risk starting little dramas that toddlers feel compelled to relive. Punishment, abuse, and emotional reactions somehow spin a story that isn't only frightening but shaming, alarming, guilt-inducing, or all of the above, even.

When your toddler goes on to push your limits, and you happen to say more than two sentences about the issue, you risk spinning them a story about a toddler with an issue — despite your attempts to remain calm while making said sentences. Maybe he held his little sister a little too tightly for the second time that week, and now he creates a connection between that and his "problem," when, in truth, it was simply an impulsive, momentary behavior.

A good example is the same one I gave about my son and my mother. My son said a curse word to my mother, who clearly indicated to me that he was unraveling. My reaction would've been a bit minimal if the rudeness was aimed at me. Instead of reacting like I did and risking spinning a story that painted him as a bad kid, I would immediately disarm those behaviors by not allowing them to affect me at all.

That said, I would certainly acknowledge the behavior. I might say, "I see you are really tired and upset. It was a really long trip." This will definitely encourage him to express his feelings even more. Always, always make it a habit to encourage your toddler to let these feelings out. And don't forget that pushing our limits with these behaviors every now and then is totally age-appropriate. If we react for too long, we just might be calling for an encore without even knowing it.

Seeing if their leaders are capable. I can imagine how unsettling it is to be a toddler and live in uncertainty about the capabilities of your leader. Even as an adult, not being certain, I have a stable leader disconcerting. The best leaders are full of confidence, a sense of humor, and an effortless attitude to work. All these qualities do not appear overnight, but not to worry, these kids give more chances than you do to get it right. They will test your limits for your own sake if that makes any sense. They just want to feel secure in your abilities. As I usually tell people, it is vital to know for sure what the priorities are for your child and for yourself, because if you seem shaky, the toddler will poke at your legs, and that will upset you. This will only emphasize the already existing problem, which in turn leads to a very sad combination of guilt, fear, and anger. Toddlers find it pretty hard being raised by equivocal parents.

A strong feeling. Toddlers are known for their persistence when testing limits because it is an outlet for them to release stress and internalized feelings. The best way for both toddler and parent to get what they want is for you, as a parent, to trust this vital process and calmly set boundaries for your toddler, while acknowledging and being accepting of his feelings. This is one of the healthiest and easiest ways to diminish his need to push your limits. I assure you, if you make your child believe that all feelings are allowed and should be expressed, you will be nipping most of these undesirable behaviors in the bud.

The purest form of flattery — kind of. By now, you should know that you are your child's most influential model. Toddlers are super sensitive, highly impressionable, and observant, so they are always on the lookout for behavior to emulate. They basically copy and reflect. A good example is when you snatch toys from your child, the tendency of that child doing the same thing to other children is very high. A toddler is likely to behave more out of control when her parents or guardians are stressed or mad about something. The likelihood of these erratic behaviors increases if the parents don't openly express these feelings.

The goal is attention. Acting out and pushing limits is pretty much the surest way to get attention these days. If you haven't been giving them as much attention or validation, or if you reacted negatively to one of her limit-pushing behaviors, which resulted in you unconsciously spinning a story that paints her bad, she is likely to repeat it to get your attention like the first time. All attention is good attention, am I right?

When last did you say, "I love you"? Toddlers love to be in their parents' good books, so when they feel even slightly ignored or out of favor, even just a tiny bit, they find it unsettling and go to fix it any way possible. What they feel is fear, so acting out is one way of releasing that emotion and expressing themselves. You need to reassure them every now and then. Hug them, kiss them, and actually say the words. All this will definitely help in rebuilding those burnt bridges. However, most love is shown through acceptance, patience, respect, empathy, and care.

Chapter Four

How to Talk to Toddlers

Toddlers are usually talked about as if they are a whole different species. If you really think about it, with all the mood swings, meltdowns, and limit-testing, it's understandable if you feel this way. But do not despair! Toddlers are just tiny little humans like you and me. The difference is that they are mostly in turmoil, and they find it difficult to maintain balance because of their rapid development, the thrill of new accomplishments, new abilities, and the frustration that comes with the realization of all they still cannot say or do. I have compiled a list of easy ways to tweak your communication skills, so communication will be much easier for you and your toddler.

Communicating with Your Toddler

Try talking normally. Toddlers are very eager to learn our languages. So instead of all the "baby talk," talk to him like you would talk to anyone else. Speak normally and in full sentences so that you are showing him a sample of what the language is and what it should sound like. Modeling the right language for your toddler right from the beginning is very important because, as I have mentioned before, they are an impressionable lot.

Speaking normally is much easier and much more natural for us. However, you should make comprehension easy by shortening the sentences, reducing the speed of your speech, and inserting a few seconds break after each sentence, so that your toddler has enough time to absorb what you said and isn't overloaded by information. I notice a lot of parents trying the Neanderthal ape talk with their toddlers as if they have some mental deficiency, and that is the only means through which babies can understand us. That ain't it, chief. Think of it this way: You're in a foreign country, and you are doing your best to learn the language. Yet, you get mocked with an imitation of your awkward pronunciations. How would you feel about that? Toddlers were not born a week ago. They have been surrounded by our language for some years now, so they actually understand way more than you think and more than they can speak.

Change that no to yes. A friend of mine, Sandra, once called me to ask for my help with a toddler problem. Her daughter — who is a year and six months old now — kept interrupting her and her husband's discussion. She told me that telling the little girl not to didn't work at all. I suggested a different approach: How about next time, she says something like, "I hear you, darling, I see you're asking for attention right now, but daddy and I are talking at the moment. When we are finished, I promise to listen to you. Give us four minutes, okay?" Then after that, mommy must follow through. This response is a magical ingredient to toddler drama. It may not work in every situation, but the truth is that toddlers never really outgrow that need for attention from their parents, even at times when you're clearly busy.

Try letting the toddler know he has been heard instead of saying "don't" and "no" every time. This shows that you respect his ego, and this is likely to draw a compliant reaction out of him. Another example is telling your child, "Please sit still on my lap" as opposed to the negative "Don't bounce on my lap!" This has been proven to reduce the toddler's urge to push limits greatly. Toddlers are thankful for positive responses and tend to act out when told "no," "don't," or any other negative word you use. I am not saying that you should eliminate the use of those words entirely. I am saying that you should just keep them in your pocket in case of emergencies.

Real choices. When you tell a toddler to put his toys away, he might resist; but when you say something like, "Are you going to put that teddy away in the box or on the bed?" you're basically giving him one of those "yes or yes" options without him realizing it. You just turned a negative into a positive, because now he gets to decide where it goes.

Another example is, "I can see that you would still like to play some more. Would you rather change your diaper now, or in about five minutes? "Making a decision between two easy options is all a toddler needs. Big questions like, "What should we get for lunch?" or "What shoe would you like to wear tomorrow?" can be somewhat overwhelming. Instead, narrow their options down to two of your choices, so either way, you both win. Another thing not to do is give false choices, like asking, "Would you like to go to

Uncle Dave's house?" It is kind of disappointing when your child says a loud no!

Acknowledge first. Acknowledgment can be calming, even for adults. When you acknowledge a toddler's point of view, you are one step closer to calming him because you're giving him the one thing he really needs: Understanding. A simple affirmation of your toddler's daily struggles is more important than you think. A good example is, "You seem to be trying really hard to put your shoes on. You're working really hard." This provides him with the enthusiasm he needs to get to the end of that stressful journey.

You should take care not to assume a toddler's feelings by saying things like, "You're scared of the cat." You should also do your best not to make your child's reaction seem invalid because you think it's simply an exaggeration. For example, "It's just a kitty; it can't hurt you "is a statement that invalidates your child's feelings. The better thing to do is only to say the things we are certain of. For example, "You seem scared of the cat. Would you like me to pick you up?" Acknowledgment takes away the disappointment of not getting their way. Here's another good example: "You want to swim in the kiddie's pool for longer, but it is time to come inside. I know it is hard to stop swimming when you're not prepared to."

Our toddler's point of view might seem wrong or plain ridiculous, but despite all this, our validation is very important to them. They need our understanding. Validating your toddler's emotions and actions means reacting to things you would rather let roll off your back. So you would say something along the lines of, "I saw you trying to run across the street. I will not allow you to do that" or, "I know you want to leave Uncle Dave's house, but it is not time just yet."

Acknowledging the emotions of a child during a very heated moment is one of the hardest things to do, besides using your tongue to touch your elbow. However, if your child chooses any moment at all to listen to you during a temper tantrum, validating his point of view encourages him to calm down. A very good example is saying, "You wanted a cupcake, and I said no cupcakes today. It is upsetting not to get your way."

Make sure your toddler feels accepted and understood, because the more she feels these things, the more she starts to understand the love and care behind all the instructions and corrections. She will still cry and resists being the toddler she is, but in the end, she is reassured that you will always be in her corner.

Chapter Five

The Toddler's Need for Boundaries

As a parent, you are going to have quite a bit of struggle with boundaries when your child starts inching closer to his first year. I've watched some toddlers climb all over their parents regardless of where they are. Why toddlers do this is because they are searching and trying to understand the boundaries and limits for their behavior. He's asking, "Where do you draw the line, daddy? Am I allowed to do this, mommy? "By not doing anything, you're doing something. You're telling them it is okay to do that. Some call it being soft-hearted; some call it fear. Some parents can't seem to say, "I do not like what you are doing right now; you can sit on me if you want, but no climbing. If you really want to climb, I'll take you to the park."

If you get started on setting boundaries and limits as early as possible, you'll give your child fewer reasons to test you. They will automatically relinquish the need to push your limits and go back to playing. I understand the fear of crushing your child's spirits and making them cry because of the many rules, but honestly, it's the exact opposite. Children will never feel fully free until someone establishes boundaries. Nobody is comfortable with that amount of uncertainty. Imagine, you just arrived at a foreign country and can't wait to explore, but you don't know the rules of the state or where you should and shouldn't go. You can't possibly explore, because you're not sure what an offense is and what is not.

Janet Gonzalez-Mena, an educator, explained the logic of establishing boundaries for kids. She said to picture yourself driving across a bridge late into the night. No streetlights or houses nearby. It is really dark. You look at the bridge and see that it doesn't have railings, what do you do? Drive across carefully and slowly. But let's say you get to the bridge and you see railings, you will get to the other side pretty confidently. This is the same way toddlers feel in regard to boundaries. Your toddler is searching for the railings. He wants to feel safe, and he will continue his limit-pushing behavior until you show him the railings.

An important part of self-development in toddlers is what we call "power struggles. This is somewhat like a fight for dominance. As an adult, you have to win, because whoever does, sets the boundaries. Children can win if you let them, and the truth is that they really do not want to. The thought of them being in charge is frightening, because now they have to set boundaries, and they do not know enough about anything to do that.

Studies have revealed that in the history of insecure and world-weary kids is an inconsistent and enabling parent. With all the burden that comes with decision making and so much power, they usually end up missing out on the joy and freedom that comes with toddlerhood.

If you attend or have attended parenting classes, you must have noticed toddlers pushing, throwing objects at people, hitting, or any other form of acting out. Parents who come to me for advice are usually the soft-hearted or scared ones, and I always advise them to do either of two things: If the parent is able to see the hit coming, they should lift their hand to intercept the hit thereby blocking the toddler's aggression, and then said matter-of-factly, "I will not allow you hit." Or if they can't anticipate the hit, right after it happens, they can say, "I do not want you hitting again." This is much better than the agitated response some parents give.

If you express anger, show agitation, or even speak too much on the matter, you put the behavior at risk of becoming a regular occurrence. For example, if a child hits during parenting classes, and the parents start to go on and on about it, saying, "Hitting is not a nice thing to do! When you hit, you hurt people! Hitting is not allowed in our family," the parent might think they're giving corrections, but what they're really doing is fueling the fire by investing more attention than necessary into the child's behavior, unconsciously encouraging the child to repeat it.

On the other hand, if the parent happens to react with "Oh no! Don't hit me, please?" or something like, "We do not hit our friends or each other, right?" the child does not quite see the railing. The boundaries are not clear. The power struggle begins as the toddler continues to push the limits to encourage the parent to take authority.

Whenever I see toddlers acting out, I picture them with little red flags in their hands that read: "Stop me! Teach me! Help me! Parent me!" As a parent, you need to react with certain clarity, confidence, and composure. If and when your toddler signals a need for limits, you need to deal with it as consistently and effectively as possible, or your child may seek other much larger red flags.

Personally, I had experienced a big red flag myself when my son and I took a walk around a park playground. A much bigger toddler who looked about five years old ran around the playground to meet us only to hit my son on the chest. He didn't cry, but he was just as shocked as I was. Then a very attractive woman rushed to me. She was the boy's mortified mother, and she couldn't find the courage to look me in the eye. She mumbled a short apology and rushed her son away.

While you need to understand and learn the best approach to toddler guidance, the complete absence of said guidance can be very consequential in the coming years. These issues left unattended can eventually lead to a destructive toddler who will only inflict pain on himself and others, causing untold damage, all as an unconscious method of seeking parental attention. The safest bet is to deal with limits and be consistent with the limits you set at an early stage. In the beginning, we all have that sweet little bundle of joy who eventually shocks us with his first show of aggression. It is shocking at first but completely normal. Every toddler will misbehave at some point, and you don't need to worry about the child being evil or having a bad future when all they're trying to do is probably tell you how tired they are and how quickly they want to get home.

Speaking of setting boundaries and how toddlers react to uncertainty and unclear power dynamics, sometimes the toddler becomes exposed to older children or even adults that do not have any respect for the child's boundaries. For example, your toddler may be grabbed and tickled when they don't want to be grabbed and tickled by anyone or at that moment. Whoever does this to them at that time has disrespected toddler's personal space or deprived her of the idea of a safe space.

When toddlers feel overpowered and assaulted in this manner, the limits already set concerning the personal space of others becomes blurry. They begin to get confused about physical limits. If, as a parent, you feel the need to roughhouse with your toddler, it is safe and advisable to wait until they are fairly old enough to be more willing to share their personal space in that way.

Imagine getting a call from your toddler's school to report bad behavior. Your initial reaction might be frustration, but if you really think about what I mentioned earlier about how a toddler's brain works and how they are constantly absorbing information in order to make sense of this world they live in, it will occur to you that they might have acted out because something at school created gaps in the railings you set up. I'll tell a short story that shows the toddler's intense need for consistent boundaries to serve as a good example.

William is a lovely, happy-go-lucky toddler who says hello to parents when they drop off their own toddlers and gives toys to other children who seem sad. One day, however, William came to school and went on to hit other children. It was very abnormal behavior for him, and his mother, Anna, was stricken with worry. I asked her if something changed at home, and she talked about how frustrating it was getting William into his car seat earlier when they needed to go somewhere. She allowed him to get into his car seat, as usual, being as patient as she could be while he spent the time playing in the car. Anna said she eventually grew impatient, and right after she told him what she'd do, she picked him up and strapped him to the car seat. The next thing that happened shocked her. He started crying so loudly. She couldn't believe it because she knew that she gave him more than enough time to get into the car seat by himself. What happened right there was that Anna pretty much confused a transitional situation. William needed to be reminded his mother was in control, and he did this by playing around, even with clear instructions hanging in the air.

I suggested that Anna pull out the yes or yes card by giving little William the option of getting into the car seat himself, but if he doesn't do it right, Anna will do it herself even if he starts screaming. Anna texted me some days later to thank me for my advice because once she made it clear that it wasn't up to him to choose to sit in the car seat or not, his need to push his mother's boundaries diminished and he stopped hitting other kids at school. The railings were restored.

Another experience that comes to mind when I think about the toddler's need for parental control oddly also enough has to do with a car seat. Sydney was a provisional mother. She carefully avoided setting limits, or if she did, they weren't permanent ones. One time she complained that she was having a hard time strapping her three-year-old daughter to the car seat. The little girl thrashed and screamed, refusing to settle down. I advised Sydney to say, "I understand that you don't want to, but you must settle down and sit in the car seat," and then go ahead to place her in the seat gently. Sydney called me some days later to give me feedback. She said that she was insistent on placing the toddler in the car seat even while she cried and hit. However, once she started the car to drive off, the child suddenly calmed down like she wasn't just acting like she felt hurt and betrayed.

Contrary to popular opinion, toddlers don't feel betrayed by their parents when boundaries are established and enforced. The little ones know that it is harder to be firm and consistent as a parent than being enabling. They may thrash around, complain, cry and throw a tantrum storm when boundaries are enforced, but deep down, they can somewhat tell when a parent is doing their best to ensure they grow in a safe and loving environment.

Chapter Six

Ditch the Distractions

A distraction is a well-known diversion trick that is invaluable when dealing with a toddler's unpleasant behavior. The reason for its consistent use is understandable because it works by shifting the focus of the child in question to another activity instead of dealing with the situation directly. It helps to avoid the sting that comes with toddler resistance, which may include tears, tantrums, a meltdown, or the silent treatment. As parents, we are more than happy to skip all of this — especially in public places. Clearly, the diversion usually works. If it did not, people wouldn't use it so often.

The thing about distractions is that they only work momentarily. I understand that it keeps you, as a parent, on the good side of things. You get to avoid being the bad guy. I absolutely hate being the bad guy too! Rather than say, "I won't let you spill water on the sofa. If you want to play with water, I will get you a water gun to play with outside," or just keep water out of their reach, I would personally choose to change the topic as smoothly as I can, because it will cause little or no friction at all. I will say instead, "Can you help me with my bag over there?" This way, I get to save my sofa from impending doom. However, the issue still remains that my child has absolutely no idea that spilling water on it is unacceptable, so he may try again much later. At least, the sofa isn't wet right now, and I don't have to deal with a sulking toddler, so I am technically still the good guy, right? This right here is the first of the many problems I have with this technique. Let's look at the rest.

The Problem with Distraction

Phoniness. I personally do not like pretending to be upbeat or perky when I'm even a tiny bit annoyed. Apart from making me look like a big faker, I don't see that as a good character to model for my children because they will pick it up eventually. Despite the discomfort that comes with facing the music or water on the sofa, I honestly think that toddlers deserve a straightforward response. This doesn't mean we are allowed to become violent in order to express our anger. If you can help it, do not react angrily. You don't have to seem chipper either, though. Learn to remain calm and give a simple but firm correction and a reasonable choice. You can say something like, "You can go play in the pool or find another thing to do," and that's all! The toddler is likely to make a face or throw tantrums as he is entitled to his feelings and conflicted opinions, but this is important. Venting is completely acceptable behavior, and our acknowledgment should come right after. You can say, "I understand that you really wanted to play with water but not on the sofa." This kind of confrontation is age-appropriate and safe for toddlers. This brings me to my second reason for not using distraction as a tool.

It takes away a learning opportunity. Toddlers need to practice ways to handle an age-appropriate disagreement with parents and other children. Whenever a toddler has a squabble with another child over a toy, the one escape parents jump at is a diversion. "Wow, take a look at this cool teddy right here!" Then the child gets distracted from the conflict, which should be considered a win... But is it really? A learning opportunity just went down the toilet. That was a good moment to educate the toddler on ways to deal with conflict by himself. A diversion to an identical toy if one is available will be helpful if the kids seem not to want to let go, but even if you provide the exact toy, your toddler might still want the one that's a little warmer in the other child's hands. Sometimes, toddlers are actually more interested in figuring out all there is to know about the current struggle than they are in the toy or whatever they seem to be struggling for. No matter what they seem more interested in, the little ones should get some time and our trust while they learn how to deal with conflicts as opposed to diversions.

Zero guidance. I need you to think really hard about this question: Do you think a child learns anything when you tell him to go get your bag just so you get him away from the couch, in the hopes that he forgets that he wanted to spill water on it? These little ones need our help understanding the rules of the house so that with time, they can internalize our values and expectations. A diversion gets rid of a possible learning moment.

It encourages a lack of awareness. Whenever you distract a child, you're basically telling him to switch gears and not remember what he literally just wanted to do. This lack of awareness is not something any parent should encourage. I recently read an article by a university press, and it said that distractions in children are really effective because of their incredibly short attention spans. So, let's say I agree that toddlers have really short attention spans (I actually don't think they do); a diversion from the activity they are currently engaged in looks like a pretty solid way to make the already short spans even shorter. Besides, some children who are used to the whole diversion tactic do not fall for it. It is going to be a little more than difficult trying to fool, lure, or coax these ones into not spilling water on the sofa, sadly. Toddlers deserve to be completely present and self-aware. They should be given a straight directive, not lured away into some other activity. The less fun part of this toddler awareness is that tricking them with the sleight of hand can prove to be quite difficult. Regardless, being attentive and aware has been proven to be a vital part of the learning process and will prove to be helpful throughout their lives.

Respect. Distraction is trickery. It's a ploy that preys on and underestimates a person's intelligence or their ability to understand and learn. When you do this to toddlers, you're basically saying they're not smart enough. Toddlers should be accorded the same respect as adults because we're all human. I saw on a website that one of the most effective forms of toddler discipline is distraction and diversion. The trick is to, first of all, take their minds off the original plan (distraction) and then put it somewhere else (diversion). The website said that a good example is suggesting they help with household chores, and in a few minutes, they will be having fun with the chores instead of putting so much emotional energy into the activity they wanted to engage in before. In my opinion, I don't understand how distraction could somehow lead to discipline. I have an important question: If you came upon two adults having an argument, would attempt to distract them by suggesting they mop up the kitchen? No? Then why do you think it is acceptable to treat a toddler the same way? I strongly believe that I can trust my child to decide where to invest his emotional energy. After all, nobody else but babies know what they themselves are trying to figure out.

Better Than Distraction

I have compiled a list of a few different responses to try instead of a distraction. These ones not only work, but they are also completely authentic and respectful:

- The first thing to do here is to breathe. Take a minute to stop and observe the situation — unless the water is seconds away from making contact with the sofa or some other disaster. If so, you should quickly grab the hands of your toddler as carefully as possible. Only then can you breathe.

- The next thing is to remain kind, understanding, and calm, but maintain firmness and consistency. If it is the issue of peer conflict, explain the situation to them from an objective point of view, and make sure not to assign guilt or blame to any one of them. This technique is called sports casting. I'll give an example: "Alice and James are struggling for the teddy and are trying really hard not to let go. It's kind of difficult when the two of you want to play with the same thing. It is giving you a hard time..." Let the struggle run its course but do not allow the children to harm each other. Say to them, "I see and understand why you are frustrated, but I will not allow you to hit."

- This next stage involves acknowledgment. You will acknowledge both feelings involved and express that you understand both points of view. "Alice has the teddy now. James, I understand you wanted it, and you are really upset that you don't have it." You need to be available and prepared to comfort the toddler if necessary — and by necessary, I mean that they request it. If it's the issue of spilling water on the sofa, you can give a response, as I mentioned above. After you have allowed the toddler to express his feelings through tears, arguments, or whatever route he takes to get it out of his system and move on, you can offer comfort and empathy if he requests it. After all that, you go ahead and acknowledge his feelings and point of view. "You felt the sofa needed to be cleaned. I didn't let you and you got upset."

- Acknowledge achievement and push more curiosity. Whenever you use distraction as a means of diverting your child's attention from one thing to another, it means you want to put a quick stop to the toddler's undesirable behaviors. Rather than do that, remember, recognize, and cheer the positive aspects of the issue. Yes, there are definitely positives. They include achievements, creativity, and curiosity. When all the tension from the situation has died down, and the lesson has hopefully been learned, you should take a moment to acknowledge the positives. "Oh my! You got on the chair to reach the shelf all by yourself. You're a big girl now." You can even let the child inspect the object and say, "Take a look at these and feel them, but I will not give them to you." If somehow it becomes a struggle, you can calmly but firmly say, "I know you really want to hold them in your hands, but I will not give them to you. I am going to stash them away high on the shelf, so you won't reach them again."

The trick here is to handle these situations whenever they arise with openness, empathy, trust, honesty, and patience. That also includes braving the tears and tantrums when then come and wearing the "bad guy" hat for a while, because the path to an understanding and loving relationship with your toddler is well worth it. This will create one of those moments you will always remember.

Chapter Seven

Why Toddlers Suck at Following Directions

I've heard a lot of parents say this one sentence: "My kids do not listen. Why? "The real thing they want to know is why their kids do not follow their instructions or directions. I'll tell you something you probably do not know about toddlers: They are more than ready to listen. They have been groomed since birth to begin deciphering the words we speak, working out our unspoken messages by instinct. This means that they understand us to some extent, right? On the other hand, these unique humans are quick to develop their own opinions, wills, and ideas. This means that they begin to think for themselves at some point. You see, toddlers understand the words most of the time. They get it. They just choose to do everything we tell them not to do. Why do they do this, you may wonder. How can they possibly understand, and then do the opposite like they didn't understand? I'll give you a few reasons for this.

Why Your Little Rascal Rebels

A feeling of disconnection. Toddlers tend to feel disconnected for a lot of reasons. Maybe you have been a bit harsh or somewhat manipulative unknowingly, instead of the well-meaning, kind, and respectful guides that our toddlers need for a better learning experience. You may have fallen into the trap of taking your toddler's age-appropriate limit-pushing behavior personally. I mean, how can this toddler for whom you'd do anything and everything for, basically give your life for, just disappoint you and fail to listen to you even after you can swear you've given that instruction about a thousand times already? You have definitely told her not to play with the electric iron, but you always find her there. You have told her not to draw on the walls, but guess what she's doing right this minute? It makes you wonder if she doesn't love you or deliberately enjoys stressing you out.

Most of the time, toddlers disobey or deliberately repeat their limit-pushing behavior when they feel like they have fallen out of favor with us. They do this when they aren't receiving as much love as they are used to. Then they get misunderstood and accused when what they're really seeking is help. Whenever we dish out a correction or form of discipline with a few drops of frustration or hostility, we risk making the little ones confused, afraid, and uncomfortable. These emotions are then manifested in their now-frequent undesirable behavior. This impulsiveness may continue for as long as we don't recognize and acknowledge the reasons for the erratic behavior. Toddlers are ready to put it on repeat until we get the message.

Your words are sometimes not enough. If your adorable toddler has ever hit you square in the face, smiles right after and hits you again, I can only imagine the look of shock the first time it happened. The first thing most parents go to say is, "Stop hurting me" or "Ouch! We do not hit." It makes you wonder if your little angel has suddenly stopped being angel-like or if he just hates you. The good news is, no, he doesn't! He is just expressing an emotion that he can't seem to put into words, and this is the perfect time to seize the moment and inform him that we completely understand and are equipped to handle the situation.

You need to show him that you've got his back. How you do this? First of all, you try holding him calmly, even if he is wiggling and wriggling. Assure him that you won't let him hit anymore because he is hurting you. If he doesn't grow calm in your arms and continues to wriggle, you can say, "You seem to be having a hard time not hurting me, so I will put you on the down." Them, follow through with your promise, even if he suddenly starts to cry.

Now that you have successfully prevented further hitting, you can now pause, breathe, and observe. Let's assume the next thing that happens is he hits you again! It is likely that your boy may not have had enough sleep last night, and despite his bedtime being a few hours away, he must be so exhausted. That's what he has been trying to tell you all that time. As a parent, it is important to understand that the use of words is not always enough for a lot of toddlers. Once you completely understand this and the difficulty in comprehending and expressing their own needs, you will begin to see how ridiculous it is when you take their disobedience or display of rebellion personally. It is up to us to express our expectations with a certain level of clarity through a firm, consistent, but kind actions.

Restraint sometimes creates guilt. When there is a conflict involving the toddler, some parents have this notion that their words should be sufficient. When they feel reluctant to follow through on what they said, they fall to pleas and appeals. This is an attempt to get the child to follow instructions or stop a particular action not out of enlightenment, but out of pity for the parents. A good example is how a parent can say, "You're hurting my feelings," when their toddler refuses to place his toys in his toy box. Some parents go as far as playing the vulnerability card, crying when there seems to be a power struggle, which, as I mentioned earlier, mostly happens when parents are reluctant to set obvious boundaries. These methods are not only fruitless, but they may also incite guilt in the toddler with a dash of a harmful sense of responsibility for the fragility of others.

We either seem way too exciting or unconvincing: I'll tell you a hard truth: If you do not really accept the rationality of a rule that you set, or if you're scared that your toddler will likely disobey, you do nothing but increase the chances of that happening.

The approach we take when giving instructions plays a big role in determining if the child will obey or not. Quite a number of parents require some help brushing up their firm and confident mommy or daddy attitude, like ending statements definitively, and not with a lilt that denotes an invisible but very obvious question mark. Instead of "Okay?" you say, "Okay."

Another skill that parents need to brush up on is a little something called the ho-hum stride. It is a perfect replacement for diving after for your toddler each time they do something you don't want them to. All the time and energy you spent chasing them around is not needed. To these toddlers, you both might just be playing a fun game, and that encourages them to keep misbehaving. The "ho-hum" method can come in handy with toddlers who scream, throw vocal tantrums, whine, or test out their newly learned cuss word on you. From my observations, toddlers are very likely not to remember the word and finally quit the whining or tantrums once we disarm the behavior but just pretending not to see it. This does not mean disregarding your toddler intentionally. You can either ignore what they're doing or simply say something really nonchalant, like "That is such an ugly word. Do not use it again," or "You are loud."

You might be over-directing. Nobody, absolutely nobody, likes being commanded around — especially the little ones, and definitely teenagers, but that's another story. If you are able to give toddlers autonomy and a chance to choose. Toddlers very much like to have a hand in their life starting from the day they are born. Let them start by making the little decisions like which shoe they would like to wear and then work your way up from there. Let them feel useful, help you solve problems, and give input in matters concerning the house.

For example, "I want to paint the living room. What do you think, white or blue?" Create a balanced environment by giving instructions and being the bad guy when needed, and spending time playing with your toddlers, letting them call the shots sometimes. This will make them more willing to listen and obey when we give instructions. Another way this tip helps is that it enables us to remember to request and acknowledge their points of view. This can be applied in a variety of situations and will help build a trusting and loving environment.

Sometimes, the toddler has better things to invest energy in. Toddler's disobedience is a good thing sometimes because it shows how healthy our toddler's amusing instinct to learn is. The best way kids do this is through curiosity, exploration, and gut feeling. My niece is about 2 years old, and each time I take her to activities like birthday parties or well-organized playgroups, she usually is not very keen on following directions. Even if she does, it happens once in a while. In the days that she does listen to instruction, she does so for a few minutes and only to a certain extent, but in general, she can be compared to a wildflower. She is the child you will find running, rolling around, jumping because she can, and dancing in the large open room while other kids are doing much more quiet activities. I wondered if I should be concerned about this or if I should just let her explore as she wants. If you have a kid like this, then you could always try to get her to settle down and pay attention to whatever it is you want her to focus on. Or, here's a better idea: You could let her have some fun doing what she wants to do. There's no harm in that.

Chapter Eight

The Art of Staying Unruffled

Toddlers have proven themselves to be masters at ruffling our feathers despite the zero disrespect they mean by that. You thought they were just disrespectful, right? Well, they were not. Pushing the limits of their parents is pretty much impulsive behavior on their part and an age-appropriate means of searching for answers to questions they consider important like: "Am I cared for? Am I secure? Are my leaders confident? Are they on my side? Are they against me? Is it right to feel what I feel or want the things that I do? Do they think I'm a bad child?"

During their search for the answers to their many questions, toddlers also use this means to reestablish boundaries and house rules. They tend to want us to clarify our expectations of them very often. A good example is," What will my mom do if I push my sister or hit the dog?" or "Will daddy be mad at me if I throw my food in the trash or take my sweet time when we're supposed to be in a hurry to leave? Should I make this decision, or should I let my parents do it? What happens if I choose to stay up past my bedtime? Can I hold mommy's hand in the grocery store? What happens if I refuse to get into my car seat?" and many more.

If we do not constantly give our toddler the reassurance or answers they require to feel safe, understood, and guided, their developing brains will push them to put their questions on repeat through their behaviors, and the more frustrated we will get. No parent can say that they have been able to ace this test every single time it comes up. We're not robots, unfortunately. We wear out, we get triggered, and this means that, every once in a while, we will lose our cool, and that is completely fine. Children will push buttons you didn't even know you had. The key is to maintain as much consistency as we can when we happen to be composed and clear. This ensures our messages get passed across efficiently.

I have a list of suggestions that I would like to share with you. What I'm about to share has helped me with my kids and has also helped the parents who have come to me for advice. Let's look at how to remain unruffled, shall we?

How to Rock the Art of Cool

Gain perspective. The way we react to our toddlers when they push our limits to determine a lot of things. Our perspective on the situation is a major definition of our attitude. When our toddlers push limits, defy us, and test our boundaries. They are giving us clear signs of their autonomy and independence. If you say blue, it is almost always required for toddlers to say green, even if their favorite color is blue. This is because if they always want the things that we want, they can't claim to be independent and autonomous individuals. All of that plus the challenges that come with a lack of control over the impulsiveness of your toddler, as well as the usual emotional instability that comes with toddlerhood, makes things a little more difficult for them and us.

This might sound a bit funny and absurd, but sometimes, I recommend perceiving these little ones more like mental health patients than misbehaved children. Toddlers clearly need our help and guidance instead of hostility and unnecessary punishments. And each time they experience fear, anger, stress, and other emotions just as strong, the likelihood of these erratic behaviors intensifying increases.

I'm never surprised when a lot of parents contact me concerning undesirable behavioral changes of their toddlers when there's a new baby, one on the way, or they are experiencing some other huge family changes the child might be reacting to. Unfortunately for the toddlers, they are not as equipped to express their feelings about these events as we are on cue. Instead of a normal conversation telling us exactly how they feel about what happened, we might get something as vague but oddly direct as "No!" in response. We get a meltdown or emotional turmoil.

Something as simple as denying them an extra cookie or something even more insignificant to us can elicit such a strong response indicating disappointment. This is why we shouldn't be quick to judge these extreme reactions but instead acknowledge and try to understand them. Rather than get offended when our toddler throws a tantrum and risk setting off a chain of similar events in the near future, you can choose to remember that this is just a means to express much deeper disappointments.

Learn to perceive strong emotions and conflict in a positive light or, at least, is a little less negative one. A lot of us were lectured as children to believe that displays of strong emotions are intolerable, and disagreements are to be steered clear of. Sadly, this view of things makes it almost impossible to remain unruffled with toddlers who, as I mentioned before, almost constantly feel the need to disagree with us and feel secure while doing so, because it is the means through which they express emotions. Working to change this pattern is one of the major challenges faced by parents, and yet it results in a more open and freeing environment.

This shift is gradually happening because each time we acknowledge our toddler's point of view, we are only reaffirming this fact. Although it seems like the last thing parents would want during a conflict with their toddler, you need to show these kids that it is completely okay for them to want whatever they want even if we don't agree and won't give it to them. Despite the ridiculousness and unfairness behind a child's opinion or choice, you shouldn't argue, judge, or coerce.

Make your expectations as reasonable as possible. Getting an overview enables us to know what to expect. This way, we won't be setting ourselves up for surprise or feel offended when our toddler does something to really annoy us, or when they flat out refuse to obey our instructions no matter how polite or reasonable they may seem, or when they deliberately disturb when we are working hard at getting dinner ready, or when they just make the most ridiculous demands. What that toddler needs is a better outlet to explode. When children go through toddlerhood, the best option is to have the most unreasonable expectations. When we expect the madness that comes with raising a toddler, it will be much easier to remain calm.

Be prepared, proactive, and preventative. You see, toddlers are wired to be curious and explorative, so putting them in environments where this is temporarily unacceptable is just setting you and the toddler up for frustration. Another thing to always remember is that children are prone to overstimulation and fatigue. Their energy levels go from a hundred to zero in very few minutes. When I say be proactive and prepared, I mean, you should always acknowledge and accept the fact that there's a huge chance your toddler will disobey or choose not to follow instructions. It's always safe to keep this in mind.

However, this should not stop you from proceeding with confidence because when giving instructions to a toddler, you need to radiate confidence to reaffirm your position on the hierarchy. This automatically means that you shouldn't give the instruction more than once since that just puts you on a path straight to anger and frustration. The healthy route for you and your toddler is to give the instruction in a way that gives the toddler a choice and enough time to save face. Don't forget, for toddlers to claim their newly found autonomy and independence; they usually need to disgrace you, the parent. Think of it as collateral damage.

The toddler codebook clearly states that obedience means weakness. You can also try plan B, the backup option, by saying something like, "Can you handle this yourself, or do you need me to give you a hand?" This clearly has nothing to do with what the toddlers can and cannot do. This is more about what they have decided to do at that moment. We have to stay prepared for when they request a helping hand because they will. This way, we can stay unruffled, show firmness, and gentleness instead of forcefulness and anger. If you anticipate willingness, you just might be disappointed. So don't anticipate it, and you'll be just fine. Also, toddlers aren't the best at putting their toys away, so they will definitely need your help or a basket, especially for that purpose. Just state your instructions in a calm but firm way, with a logical consequence. For example, "I won't let you take out any more teddies until we put these into the toy basket."

Act as if. Another important part of the parenting approach I practice and teach is the authenticity of a parent. It is clear that dealing with toddler behavioral problems using a non-punitive approach is a highly important and respectful goal that, oddly enough, doesn't seem to occur to a lot of parents. Either way, acting as if it is another way to achieve this. When I encourage parents to act as if they are unruffled, I don't mean to tell them to put on stern voices and faces or pretend to laugh or play games. What I mean is, imagine you've been handling situations like this for so long that you've mastered the art of remaining completely calm and laid back. This way, being definitive and direct comes easily to you, and you can follow through when it's necessary. As soon as you see how effective this method is, you can begin work on building real confidence, so you need to act as if anymore.

The use of imagery. We all have that one or list of pictures that make us feel calm and comfortable. Print that image if it isn't framed already or keep it somewhere easily accessible. Use the image to remain calm and secure when building your confidence or staying unruffled under toddler pressure. This image can also provide the tiny emotional distance you will need at this time.

Practice. One truth remains: It definitely gets better and easier. With every small win, your confidence gets an insane spike, and this makes it easier for you to get into character better than you used to. You will find it much easier to express your personal boundaries, and this confidence spreads to have a positive effect on other relationships you may have.

Be on the lookout for personal triggers, weaknesses, and projections. When you practice self-reflection, it enables you to discover your buttons almost as seamlessly as your toddler does. When you do this, the next step is to understand them because only then can they be dis-empowered. Recognition is stepped one on the path to change and dis-empowering your triggers. Doing this for the sake of your child has an immense healing effect.

Find support. Dealing with a toddler is a very intense life experience. To remain unruffled in the presence of the little ones doesn't involve seeming unruffled to everyone else. Find someone to talk to, a shoulder to cry on; a means to vent. If necessary, get a counselor or sign up for therapy. Don't be afraid or ashamed to get the help you need. It doesn't make you a bad parent. It makes you the ones who love their toddler enough to want to raise them in the best way possible.

Chapter Nine

The Toddler's New Baby Blues

One time, I had just landed at the airport and was calmly waiting for my luggage at the baggage claim carousel when my ears caught wind of a heated exchange. I searched for the source of the ruckus, and I found it right at the adjacent carousel. Standing, there was a little boy about three or four years old dressed in a brightly colored traveling outfit. He looked to be searching for something in his striped backpack while his father stared daggers at him and screamed, "Why can't you be nice to your sister? Just be nice to her!"

A few feet away, I saw his mother so glaring at him while she held a 12-month-old baby (I guessed) in her arms whom I assumed to be the baby sister being talked about. This little boy remained as composed as he could be, but did everything to avoid his parents' gaze. At that moment, he seemed vulnerable, and so alone. The black sheep. A problem child no longer in favor of his family. It made me wonder if this little scene I just witnessed was a regular occurrence in that family. If so, then I couldn't imagine that little boy ever directing any emotion besides bitterness towards his little sister.

I don't think anything exists that creates the kind of emotional turbulence created by the impending arrival or birth of a baby brother or sister. The severity of the changes caused by this single event in a family is mostly felt very deeply by the youngest, most sensitive, and vulnerable member despite the level of awareness, care, and sensitivity possessed by the parents. It is responsible for all sorts of changes, behavioral and emotional, like extreme mood swings, severe limit-pushing behavior, and a slight or major regression in development.

Each time I am contacted by a parent concerning a sudden and extreme behavioral shift in their toddler, I play detective, asking as many questions as I need to figure out the recent major changes that might have taken place and how they affect the family dynamics. When it seems to be taking too long, and I already have a pretty solid idea of what the problem might be, I ask a pretty straightforward question: "Has any major change occurred in the past month or past few weeks?" More often than not, I usually get an affirmative. It usually sounds something like this "Err, we just had a new baby…" or "I'm right around my due date…" and that is all I need to know to understand why the child has taken to extreme measures to express his sadness about the situation.

I have come up with a list of certain key points to remember when dealing with toddlers during such a major adjustment. Let's take a look:

Dealing with Adjusting Toddlers

Make sure your expectations are reasonable. This is important despite how badly your toddler must have wished for a baby sister or brother, because as soon as the new baby arrives and your attention shifts (and it will), reality will hit and it will hit hard. This shift in affection will be felt as deeply as a loss by the toddler. Children feel a wide range of emotions like sadness, guilt, grief, and even anger, but the one that hits closest to home is the fear of losing their parent's affection. When this happens, they become overwhelmed by this raging blend of feelings, of which they probably understand only half. They feel like they're sinking in a sea of emotions that they definitely can't articulate. So they find an outlet, and most of the time, it's the least amusing kind.

Acting out their sadness and disappointment through limit-pushing behavior that turns aggressive sometimes is one of the ways they tell you they don't feel very good. Mood swings take a turn for the worst, becoming more extreme than you've seen them. You might even be surprised to uncover a bad side to your child that you never knew they had. The shock even intensifies if the toddler was expected to be a helpful, adoring, and loving big brother during the difficult change, especially if he whined about having a baby brother for some time now. Behaviors like these are the kind that pushes our buttons, but the emotions you will feel as a parent in response to these behaviors shouldn't be expressed with hostility and extreme punishment because now more than ever, your toddler needs your reassurance, empathy, and love during this emotional crisis.

Always encourage children to express their emotions. There are a few vital means through which parents can assist their toddlers in expressing their emotions in the healthiest manners. When the toddler begins to act out with the new child, giving the baby uncomfortable kisses, tapping the baby too hard, or even jumping dangerously close to where the baby is being laid, you must take action. Once you calmly but firmly set the boundaries as I mentioned in chapter five, you can ask a no-nonsense question like, "You're feeling rather rough towards your little sister now, aren't you?" or "You seem upset about your little brother is here. Are you? It's okay for big sisters to feel like that sometimes, but right now, I am going to get you down from the bed. Why don't you come to perch on my lap if you want? Or you can just play around on the floor right beside me."

Try casually talking about the reason behind all the negative feelings at often as you can. "I understand how hard it is to be a have a baby sister. It's okay to get upset with the baby or daddy or mommy too. It is normal to feel sadness, worry, or just be angry and not be able to figure out why. Anytime you feel any of these emotions; I want you to be able to talk to me about them. I always promise to love and understand you. I would really like to help you." It may seem illogical to suggest these emotions to your impressionable toddler because it just might encourage him to develop ill feelings towards the newborn, right? However, that's not how it works. If you openly acknowledge and welcome your toddler's negative feelings and thoughts, the chances of those emotions clearing up to reveal a genuine bond between him and his new sibling.

Bringing up negative emotions when the toddler looks okay. It is possible for a toddler to adapt seamlessly and peacefully to the new changes that a newborn brings. There is no point in projecting emotional problems that don't exist, right? I'll tell you why you should at least try, even if your child seems fine. In my opinion, toddlers who are readily open-minded and accepting of this huge adjustment in the family tend to require even more reassurance of affection and more inspiration to open up about any negative emotions they may feel about the situation. They need this more than the toddlers that immediately wage war. Despite the amount of positivity any change contains, you will always find trace amounts of loss and fear lurking somewhere. This doesn't just apply to toddlers; it affects adults too. If these emotions aren't acknowledged and duly expressed, they become internalized. Your toddler may be well behaved during this period, but there's a good chance she has pent up negative emotions.

Stay away from comments that induce guilt: When a family is expecting the arrival of another baby, relatives and friends usually drop guilt-inducing comments on the first child but not out of spite. They might say things like, "I bet you just can't wait to meet your baby sister, am I right?" However, long before then, it would've already dawned on the toddler that being the "big brother" or "big sister" isn't all sunshine and rainbows like the relatives paint it. Before then, they have realized the shift of attention from them to the child that hasn't even arrived yet. The future seems full of uncertainty to them, and in their heads, it is bound to get worse. What they need during this time is someone understanding who will reassure them of the constant inflow of their parents' affection and attention. Someone who will untangle their mixed feelings and let them know that, however, they feel about the situation is valid, but everything will be okay. If this emotional shoulder to cry on isn't made available, the toddler is likely to internalize these feelings and even develop resentment towards a sibling that hasn't even been born yet.

Put your judgment hat away. As I said before, this is about regulating our expectations and understanding the fact that limit-pushing behaviors are only an outlet for the child to express his confusion and sadness. Each time we place a label on certain behaviors, children tend to feel judged, and they take this judgment very seriously. Judgments like "mean!" "Bad!" "Not nice!" can be taken a little too personally by toddlers. They feel like it's not just the behavior that's bad, it's them too. These judgmental words are even absorbed more if they're being said by someone they trust and love most in the whole world. If you tell your toddler that he is not a good boy, he will believe you, and the next emotion to follow is deep rejection.

Reduce tension by not dwelling on insignificant things. Being a second child is considered more exciting than being a first child because there's an older sibling involved. Such luck. Second born's are brought into a very different world from the ones their older sibling grew up in because they get to have a big sister or brother. Knowing this, if you can help it, leave it alone. Let them make so much noise, let them create chaos, and allow more interference to the newborn's playtime. Allow big brother to collect toys from the little one during playtime together but only as long as he does this in a physically safe manner. As a parent, you should understand how powerful and symbolic that impulse it. It is, in fact, the symbol of rivalry felt by the older child. A lot of babies don't have a problem with sharing their toys or having the toys taken from them unless it's their parents. Dd. Anyway, the more you choose to focus on other things instead of these harmless behaviors, the less the chances of the older sibling repeating them.

Make peace with your child's need for autonomy and trust. Feel free to ask your toddler for help whenever necessary, especially when it has to do with the newborn's care. Whenever their emotions are going haywire, these little chances for autonomy have a certain calming effect. However, don't feel disappointed when your child refuses to help you out because defiance is also a form of autonomy, and we're all for that, aren't we?

Squeeze in some one-on-one time. Creating space in your day for some alone time with all your children is more important than a lot of parents realize. Keep in mind that the quality of the time spent, not the quantity is what matters to your toddler and the newborn Try to carve out about 20 or 30 minutes each day that you dedicate solely to your toddler. This might require you to put the new baby to bed much earlier than usual, but it is well worth it. During those 20 or 30 minutes, you will be wholly focused on your toddler. Now when you have to focus on the newborn and your notice your toddler struggling, all you have to do is acknowledge the emotion, saying, "I can see how unsettling it is for you when I am feeding your sister. It's really difficult for you, I know, but I am really looking forward to our mommy-daughter time together right after I put your sister to bed. I'd like you to come up with ideas for what you'd want us to do together." And that's how you defuse a bomb!

Push for the newborn's independent playtime. Having a baby who can entertain himself is the best thing that can happen to any parents who already have a child. This is because the parents get to have time to be with the older child during baby self-play hours. Having the baby between you and your toddler every time, especially when the toddler hasn't fully accepted the new situation, can create some friction. Encourage the baby's independent playtime. Prepare a safe and confined play space like a playpen or a crib (these are perfect during the first few months) so that you don't have to constantly supervise the baby while you spend time with the older child. It is also advisable to set boundaries concerning the baby's playtime because your toddler might need to see some railings as he might feel compelled to push your limits by disturbing the baby.

Your toddler will continue to need you even after he goes a rank higher to older brother: Even after having another child, your duty to your toddler still continues. You will still be needed to set boundaries, and you have to respect and honor this need. You will still continue to play the role of the calm and helpful parents who have their back. I understand that doing this might be a little too exhausting, and for this reason, you might have to cut back on the boundaries. However, your toddler still requires the affection and security that comes with your boundaries even more now. They will require you to give them no-nonsense reminders like "Make sure you do not touch your sister when you're feeling uneasy for some reason." They will also require you to drop choices like, "I will let you stay here beside me quietly while I place your sister in her cot. If you won't be quiet, go, and play in the sitting room." When required, you will need to gently but firmly follow through physically by removing them from circumstances. More importantly, your toddler will need you to intervene long before you even think of losing their temper or telling them they are "mean." This intervention should take place with all the empathy, confidence, patience, and calmness you have in you.

Chapter Ten

The Truth about Consequences

Doing a routine check within ourselves to answer a very vital question is really helpful when steering through the part of being a parent associated with the discipline. The question "What are ideal parenting goals?" is more important than people know when dealing with toddler discipline. If the base goal is ensuring a lasting bond with your toddler, then phrases like "Get this concept into his small head" or "Get her to do this and that, make him get that" and so on are obvious signs that we have gone off track.

What Makes Consequences Fail

When on the path of disciplining your toddler, do not start from a place of manipulative behavior. It will not serve you well, and it won't serve you for long. This will constantly threaten your authority as a parent because it gives rise to some friction in the relationship you have with your toddler as opposed to the healthy partnership that toddlers require for adequate guidance. Despite the importance of consequences when practicing respectful toddler discipline, consequences fail to be fully effective when:

They become a substitute for penal discipline. Punishments have proven to be successful deterrents for an unwanted behavior, but more often than most parents would like to admit, punishments give rise to more punishments in the future. I consider punishments to be ineffective when it comes to instilling discipline because they don't exactly scream positivity. Punishment is a negative reaction to bad behavior. Remember what I said about toddlers and negative behavior? Punishments tend to also come with a bag full of unintended and unfortunate consequences. Punishments give toddlers a reason to internalize anger, disappointment, shame, and other strong negative emotions out of fear of being punished.

Punishments do well to create a rift between parent and child. It pushes the child into a life of isolation, secrecy, and mistrust. Some punishments come with such severity that it creates rage, hopelessness, fear, and intense helplessness. A Psychologist called Paul Bloom is an expert on baby and toddler studies. He conducted some research on the level of understanding possessed by toddlers, and he discovered some fascinating stuff. Toddlers have a good enough understanding of fairness. This means they can tell when they're being treated fairly, and when we're just mean. If you dole out respectful consequences to your toddler, it will register somewhere in their brain, and they will acknowledge our fairness, but this does not automatically mean that there won't be any objections since objection is the toddler's game. There 2ill be disagreements despite the degree of fairness, and this defiance needs to be acknowledged. Toddlers tend to trust us more when they sense sincerity and fairness in our dealings with them. If they trust us already, it becomes even stronger. Punishment is just pettiness. You don't want your child to perceive you to be petty, do you? They might not know the exact word, but they will know that there is definitely something odd about mommy or daddy.

Punishments are sometimes completely unrelated to the circumstances involved or doled out long after the issue has passed or been resolved. There are so many inspiring things about kids, but the most inspiring is their ability to exist at the moment. Once a thing happens and is settled, they are quick to move on. The younger the toddler, the easier it is for them to let go, and soon enough, they won't be able to understand the reason why they're being punished because they already let the issue go as you should! Each time your toddler defies boundaries you clearly set up, it is wise to deal with it as quickly as it happens and join our kids on the moving train. Don't dwell, brood, seethe, or hold grudges. Your child is likely not to remember, so you'll end up confusing or hurting him with your negative expressions.

If you really think about it, this situation could've been prevented or avoided if you set a clear limit or put up a boundary. As a parent, it is your job to avoid circumstances that are likely to cause conflict. If you have older children, urge them to protect their valuables like projects, electronics, and others from the toddlers who, at their level of development, care only about exploring. Hide your important things too on high places like shelves and cupboards, so you have no reason to get upset for any damages done. It is unfair for you to let a destructive event happen when you could've prevented it. It saves you a lot of time and negative emotions.

Punishments are very attached to forced feelings of remorse and inauthentic apologies. When you punish a child, they are forced to say anything to end their suffering, and anything can include false apologies. Each time you induce a false apology or render false forgiveness, you risk teaching your toddler a few unproductive things like pretending to do and feel things in order to get favor from adults, a complete lack of trust in their true feelings, using "I'm sorry" when they do not mean it or as an excuse. You may not know it, but you're teaching your child to be a phony.

There are a few ways through which consequences can be made to be respectful and effective while fostering the relationship between parent and child. Let's take a look.

Beneficial Consequences

Be sure to give the toddler reasonable, logical, and age-appropriate choices. You should always keep in mind the age and capabilities of your toddler. You cannot set unreasonable options before him and get upset when he picks one that you consider undesirable. You can say something like, "I will not let you throw these blocks towards the mirror. You seem to be having a hard time not throwing the blocks at the mirror. If you really want to throw blocks, throw them towards the carpet or into the basket. If not, I will have to put them back into the toy box." If he defies you, follow through by saying, "Thank you for informing me that you need my help. I will take the blocks away and put them in the box now," and please put them in the box despite the whining and crying that may follow.

State the consequences kindly but sternly. Most parents resort to making threats instead of stating the consequences. Your toddler is not a criminal, so go ahead to state the punishment matter of factly then immediately let it go and carry on. For a lot of parents, this means that they have to put these boundaries in place as early as possible so that you don't put yourself in a position where you have to speak to your child in anger or frustration.

Don't forget always to acknowledge your child's point of view. I have mentioned this earlier and how important this is. With regard to giving consequences, you need to respect the child enough to acknowledge their point of view, no matter how ridiculous it may seem. This way, the child has a better understanding of how their thinking is flawed and might be less likely to defy you. You can say something like: I know you really wanted to stay and play at the park, but I saw that you had a difficult time not hurting your friends, so I decided to take you home. I see how sad you are."

Resort to predictable responses, consistency, and elements of a routine recognized by the child. You can say something along the lines of "Are you done with your food? You seem to be standing up, so I think it is safe to assume you are finished eating. Okay, you're going to sit back down so you can eat some more. Please do not stand up unless you want to tell me you're done, and I will put the remaining food away." If he gets up after that boundary has been set, you have to follow through by putting the food away. "Thank you for letting me know that you are finished eating. You are sad that I put your food away. You didn't really like that, and I understand. It will be time for dinner soon."

A real expression of our own limits. This is usually where my fellow respectful discipline advocates clash. This is where I draw my own boundaries. There was a time that a good friend of mine, who couldn't have been a more caring, respectful, and all-round super mom, attended a parenting class held by a well-known calm parenting adviser. My friend's biggest hurdle when it came to parenting, was setting proper limits. She was a provisional mom. She was highly susceptible to feelings of self-doubt and guilt if the circumstances affect her personal limits or aren't as distinct as a safety issue.

She went on to ask the parenting adviser about some experience she had a while go when she was driving her 5-year-old son to a friend's house for a birthday party. She said that her daughter got very angry with her baby brother and would not stop yelling. My friend said she patiently tried appealing to her to stop yelling a couple of times, but it fell on deaf ears. My dear friend was getting very frustrated and losing her patience very quickly. She then asked the parenting adviser if it would've been okay for her to have told her daughter that they would turn back right then and head straight home if she stopped screaming. The adviser looked her dead in the face and said no. According to the adviser, it would have been a consequence imposed by a parent.

I won't lie, the moment I heard that, I thought I would lose it. My friend was one of the many moms around the world who needed to be encouraged to set boundaries and take charge at home, but rather, she was being reprimanded for simply suggesting it. Oddly enough, this parenting adviser claimed to specialize in assisting parents in their journey to a 'no yelling' household, but for some reason, managed to miss a vital piece of the puzzle. Parents require a lot of encouragement from friends and family to ensure that they properly take care of themselves in the best way they can in order for them to build honesty, confidence, calmness, and fairness, and also so that they are not a ticking time bomb around their kids waiting to explode. The truth, however, remains that there are some people that believe that parents need permission to set limits on their toddler taking out more toys from the toy box even when they haven't cleared up the toys from yesterday. They clearly need permission to decide to go straight home instead of a birthday party if their toddler won't stop yelling. They need permission to choose to go to the grocery store alone if their child refuses to put on their clothes. Parents should be allowed to say things like, "I know you wanted you to play with your other toys today, but we had an agreement. If you don't put the ones on the carpet back in the box, I won't allow you to use these ones." Or, "You said you felt like accompanying me to the grocery store today, but I don't have a lot of time so please put your clothes on or do you need my help?" or "I can see that you very sad about missing the birthday party but you wouldn't stop yelling, and I told you. I know I did". You see, the major difference between punishments and consequences is the honesty and sincerity behind our sharing. You can't be gentle and respectful parents without properly taking care of ourselves first.

When Parents Disagree

Disciplining children can be placed on the same ranks as money when talking about causes of disagreements between parents, probably because of how important, stressful, and relentless it is. The conflict caused by different opinions harbored by parents on the issue starts to rear its ugly head during the period a child goes through the toddler stage. This happens because, during this period, both parents feel this heightened need to become disciplinarians. They both have ideas for how they want their children to behave.

Disputes surrounding this usually come as a surprise to parents who felt they knew all there is to know about each other. However, no matter how much you think you know your partner, you cannot avoid conflict, especially when it comes to the manner with which to raise your child. Besides, there isn't a place where two people are on the same page about everything. Once child discipline comes into the picture, everything becomes a factor: Relationships, temperaments, family background, personal outlook on life, and so on. These factors come into play to determine the level of expectations and responses.

Imagine a situation where you totally think a timeout is the right course of action because your child just spilled all his tea on the floor just because he requested another cup, and it wasn't given to him. Your partner doesn't agree with you, and instead finds the behavior pretty amusing. Or, how about a scenario where the conflict gets a little heated, and there is an argument about the pros and cons of spanking? That wouldn't be very nice, especially if it happens right in front of the toddler. As expected, I have a list of suggestions to help you deal with conflicts that concern child discipline.

1. **Keep up a unified front.** The first and most important thing about arguments like this is that they should never happen in front of your toddler, no matter what. Bearing witness to a fight between mommy and daddy can make the child feel insecure and uneasy. You might think they're too young to know what's going on, but a child as young as 12 months old can tell when there's discord between parents. Arguing about discipline in front of your toddler can give him the sense that it is all about him, and his brain automatically makes him think that he is the reason why mommy and daddy are fighting even when that is not the case. Children are drawn to the affection of both parents like a moth to a flame, and they will do anything to get it. They are naturally mommy and daddy pleasers, and witnessing a fight over discipline can make them feel like they have displeased one or both parents somehow. Open conflict like that also sabotages any attempts made to handle the problem. Also, toddlers being the sneaky creatures they are, are likely to break the rules or cross boundaries the exact way much later because he senses a weak link between mommy and daddy, so he's likely to get away with it. The way to go about this is to let the parent who was already started on the situation to finish

handling it, then the two of you can settle your differences after you put the child to bed.

2. **Be understanding and acknowledging of your different parenting styles.** We all have that one parent who is more lenient or stricter than the other. Your family background and how you were raised by your parents play a huge role in influencing your behavior as a parent and a disciplinarian. Some experts say that the family background of a parent influences their parenting skills, especially punishments and mealtimes. Talk to your partner. Discuss each other's life lessons, philosophies, search for compromises, settle on middle ground, recognize and accept the things that may never really agree on, and trust your partner. I know that no parent should be left out of child discipline, but to avoid major arguments, the parent that spends more time with the toddler should be the one to decide the general tone so that the toddler does not get confused at any point. An exception to this suggestion is when said parent's actions start to get emotionally, verbally, and physically abusive. That shouldn't be tolerated.

3. **Don't attack.** Instead, persuade, there is nothing as offensive as hearing your partner belittle or criticize your methods of handling a situation. Nobody gets on the defensive faster than a parent whose mode of discipline is being attacked, especially for no reason. When dealing with your partner, try to word your feelings in a more positive manner. You can say something like, "That is how I handle situations like that, and this is why it always works no matter what." Another thing to do is

acknowledge that your way isn't the only way. There are a thousand right ways to do things, especially child discipline. Whatever you do, try not to assume that your way is absolute and law. A lot of parents fall into this trap of making their word on toddler discipline law because they're the ones who spend most of their time caring for the child. That is just setting yourself up for disagreement. What you should do instead is ask yourself why you believe that your method works best, talk to your partner about it, discuss the reasons why you both think your methods have the child's interest at heart and decide on the best solution which might end up being a combination of both your approaches. Whatever you do, don't feel threatened by the appearance of another approach and the likelihood of it working even better than yours. Always remember, the child comes first, not your ego. Even if both of you have very effective approaches and the arguments are starting to look like a struggle for dominance rather than a search for a proper disciplinary solution, one of you to concede to keep the peace.

4. **Search for the cause.** Some other effective way to move from attacking each other to searching for a solution to the problem is to find out the reason for the disagreement. Maybe the father is more sensitive to a cry for even the most ridiculous reasons, unlike his partner. A lot of differences in points of view of the partners can be traced to one or both of them having unreasonably high expectations. A good example is when a father who thinks that a toddler at 18 months old should not still be using a bottle at that age, whereas the mother does not see a problem with that habit. Do your best to see beyond the surface

of the disagreement in order to discover the reason why you and your partner feel the way you do. Another important thing is to be as specific as you can be. Do not beat about the bush or run around in circles because that is just prolonging the real issue and ensuring the thinning of you and your partner's patience. Besides, it is wiser and far more useful to keep your discussion confined to a specific issue instead of generalizing and possibly hurting feelings in the process. Something like, "You let Sarah eat whenever she wants "is better than" Why you find ways to undermine my authority?" I'm sure you can see the difference.

5. **If possible, agree to disagree.** No matter what you and your partner do, there's a likelihood of you two not coming to an agreement on every aspect of your toddler's upbringing. You don't have to see eye to eye or impose your ideas, and neither do they. Toddlers are flexible and smart enough to know who they get what privileges from. Daddy always buys them candy, but mommy thinks it is bad for their teeth, or it's easier to get mommy to squeeze in an extra bedtime story than daddy. Tiny differences in opinion will not confuse your child. If anything, it does more to educate your child on individuality and how different personalities respond to different situations. All you need to make sure of is that you are completely supportive of each other and unified in front of the toddler. When the big problems arise, like an appropriate punishment for biting or stealing, you and your partner have to come together to arrive at the best possible course of action. The most important person in all of this isn't you or your partner. It is your child.

Conclusion

We have finally arrived at the end of this book, and I hope you have found it inspiring and enlightening! The exact routes you will take to mold your child's behavior will vary in a million ways, and these variations depend on certain factors like the child's age, emerging toddler personality, the circumstances involved, where you and the child are, and even the time of the day. Before I wrap up this book, I would like to leave you with some golden rules that can help you lay the foundation of the overall journey to loving but effective toddler discipline.

Don't forget to highlight the positive. It must seem pretty easy to fall into the habit of only reacting to your toddler, always coming to intervene with a truckload of corrections behind you when something goes wrong, no matter how insignificant. However, I can assure you that you'll record much more success if you search for situations that give you the opportunity to praise your toddler's good behavior. Parents need to support good behavior actively. If you're at this point in this book, you probably already know that your child places your approval and affection above everything else. Nothing else matters more, not even food. This is why positive words of encouragement and appreciation every now and then are a much better and healthier teacher than other negative methods of discipline.

Don't be stingy with hugs. Your child loves them! Hug your toddler when she exhibits good behavior no matter how seemingly negligible. Give praises and compliments in a special way when it is needed. You can say, "I really like how you arranged your toy boxes on the shelf when you were done with them." Don't make your toddler resort to limit-pushing behavior before you think you shower attention.

Pace your child every now and then so that he doesn't begin to feel frustrated or overtired. When the signs of sleep start to peek through, there should be a complete gear change for either a nap, quick snack, or totally different activity before you experience a total meltdown courtesy, your toddler.

Another really important thing that I will probably repeat because I honestly can't stress this enough is to show your toddler some respect. Whatever effort you do works to create a lasting sense of security and self-confidence. You will also notice the lessened overall need for constant intervention.

As often and efficiently as you can, try to prevent problems. Toddler-proof your home when you have the time. This automatically eliminates the untouchables from your child's immediate environment, and if he doesn't touch an untouchable, you won't have any reason to chastise him. Another way of preventing problems is deliberately avoiding situations that you know will stir up trouble. Situations like trying to get one more errand in when it's already way past his nap time, or taking your hungry toddler past the checkout counter filled with candy at the grocery store without getting her any. If you are fully aware that your toddler is incapable of sitting still in a diner, why would you even take her there when there's always the option of ordering takeout instead?

Get rid of the exhausting struggles over inappropriate clothing by stashing away the clothes for winter in a place the child doesn't know or can't reach yet when in summer. Reverse this during winter for summer clothes.

Another healthy way to reduce the likelihood of a tussle is to give your toddler fair warnings before things begin to head south. Toddlers are highly dependent on rules and boundaries because of their short memory span. They need to see those "railings" as constantly as you can make them available. A good example is dropping a reminder right before a bath. Take his clothes off in preparation for the bath and right before you dip him in the water, say matter-of-factly, "You know how we do this. If you splash, I will take you out of the water, and that is the end of the bath, complete or not." or when you give her a cookie and remind her that the rule says we only eat in the kitchen.

Set reasonable limits. Every toddler needs his parents to set boundaries. Living with a toddler requires setting and reinforcing boundaries every now and then. These boundaries must be consistent, crystal clear, and in abundance. As I have mentioned before, toddlers need these boundaries in order to feel safe in their environment. Limits tell your child what mommy and daddy don't like, so it becomes easier to filter out what they do like. Limits spell out acceptable and unacceptable behavior for the children, and these limits are more reassuring than we realize. Your toddler understands more about boundaries by watching your cues, listening to your spoken reminders, and by limit-pushing behaviors. Initially, setting and reinforcing rules may not exactly seem like the most important thing to do because it doesn't really harm anyone if or when your 12-month-old shreds every single paper he comes in contact with or if your 2-year-old does not say please for anything. The truth is that your reactions to those situations help to determine your child's behavior in the future. If you refuse to disapprove of behavior as soon as you notice, no matter how absolutely cute your child looks while he defies you, you won't think it's so cute or comical anymore when you experience it an extra dozen times. This means that you will have to make a decision about your feelings when it comes to the chain of mischief that will occur once your toddler begins to explore and understand our world. He is just testing out things to see which ones are acceptable and which ones are not, and it is your duty to inform him. A lot of parents make the mistake of ignoring certain toddler misbehavior, saying, "But he's just a sweet little guy, there's no way!" or "He can't possibly understand when I say no." But! Toddlers are smarter than you give them credit for so. However, with your guidance and understanding, it is possible for them to learn well from the bad.

Don't be scared to be firm. Some parents make the costly mistake of sticking to the easygoing end of discipline. This usually happens because they remember how much they hated all the rules and regulations as a child, so they decide not to let their children go through what they went through. Another reason parents choose the less firm approach is the fear of spoiling a good time. They get so focused on the good times that they do not wish to spoil it with a negative reaction, so they end up shoving that response where the sun doesn't shine, and there goes yet another missed learning opportunity.

It is completely understandable to want your toddler to have and enjoy a good time, especially the ones they have with you. Playing the adult and parent is a role dreaded by so many parents. Especially the new ones who are still coming into their role, the divorcees that don't have full custody of the child, or parents who unfortunately work very long hours. Indulgence has a special spot in parenthood that goes without saying. So does give your toddler a reasonable amount of freedom. However, this should only exist together with clearly laid out boundaries that most of these parents do not realize that parenting with a lack of firmness eventually backfires over time. If you don't put those railings in place, you are robbing your toddler of an understanding of your expectations. Instead of the freedom this lack of firmness should bring, the exact opposite tends to take place: This lack of boundaries moves unsettles your toddler.

Parents who refuse to be firm end up dealing with more disciplinary issues. Also, children who grow up with overly indulgent parents tend never to understand the importance of taking responsibility for their own actions and granting respect and acknowledgment of other people's feelings. If you're too soft-hearted, your child will see an opportunity to take advantage of you and will take it. It is the power struggle I spoke of earlier. Soon enough, he will uncover all your buttons and begin work on learning how to push them to give undesirable responses to you. This behavior will continue until you've had enough and finally decide to set rules. He will push and push and push until little problems become major disasters. It is better and healthier for both of you that you make it clear from the beginning that you run the family, not your toddler. If you try to do this later, it will work, but it will be much harder than it would've been if you started early.

A great misconception is that firmness equals effective discipline. This misconception leads parents to become the humorless, rigid commander at a junior boot camp. Yes, the other extreme has its own risks, which is why balance is important. It is possible for you to be rigid as a parent, all in the name of firm discipline. Parents like this set boundaries so wide that it affects every single aspect of the toddler's life, leaving little or no room for autonomy, and even worse, they go on to enforce every single one of those rules. Parents who are authoritarians are usually perfectionists and control freaks. They mostly lack any patience in understanding the special mindset of a toddler. Instead, they lean heavily on the because-I-said-so approach to discipline.

Parents like this tend to lean heavily on tactics such as intimidation, screaming, hostility, fear, etc. Most authoritarian parents were probably raised in similar environments and under similar leadership. Regardless, going too hard on firm discipline when molding your child's behavior means that you risk making it worse than it should be. It works to build a clashing relationship between parent and child, which is hardly conducive for imparting knowledge.

Inflexibility with your toddler also works to reduce his inborn curiosity and might greatly affect his self-esteem and confidence in later years. Maintaining a delicate balance between firmness and leniency is usually the best option. Showing respect to your child's need for autonomy and freedom is as important as helping him grow in confidence, respect, and an understanding of how the world works. Love and limits can coexist.

Always have realistic expectations. Believe me when I say that you will be setting yourself up for disappointment and failure if you're always setting the standards unreasonably high with regards to your toddler's behavior. If you're always aiming at one unrealistic goal or another, you will be disappointed a lot. 12-month-olds can hardly sit at a spot for up to twenty minutes, but you want your toddler to sit still at the dinner table with the entire family for one hour? Let's be real here; you will be feeling a lot of frustration that night. A two-year-old can't physically manipulate the workings of bed-making on her own, but you feel she should arrange her room every morning? What I advise is you get some information, whatever you can, on toddler development so you can have an idea of what is possible and what is not. You can carefully raise your expectations as your toddler grows.

The goal is consistency. The minute you make a new rule, remember to reinforce it every now and then because toddlers find inconsistency confusing. Another thing you should do is be as straightforward as you can get to avoid any misconceptions. Your child might be wondering why she could have a cookie yesterday, but not today. If it was okay to leave the toys out of the box yesterday, why is daddy so upset about it today?

Thoughts like this confuse toddlers, and so many of them don't have the means to express themselves using direct words, so it is up to you to avoid as much toddler confusion as you can by following through on your limits in a fairly predictable manner. If you say you will seize the toys for a few days if they forget to put it back into the box, then don't forget to do so. If you say you will leave the store without any treats, if they hit down any goods at the grocery store, don't get them any treats if they disobey. Don't allow him to think it is okay to get away with defiance every time. It may seem like a negligible deal, but the next time you give that same rule, you won't be taken very seriously, and you shouldn't be because you have shown in the past that you don't say things that you mean. Both mommy and daddy should put on a generally consistent and united front in all things. It will definitely be unrealistic of me to expect 100 percent consistency every time in every aspect. I expect the exceptions because they will happen, and you don't have to beat yourself up about it. You are doing just fine. An example is when you let your toddler jump up and down on the sofa when she has been cooped up inside the house for a while due to rain or excess snow. You can also let her have her snacks in the bedroom if you have business partners over. Sometimes, you might be too tired after a long day at work to complain about the toys she left out of the box, but that's okay, you will get to it after a good night's rest. Don't forget to give an explanation for the deviation for the day so that they don't feel confused and test your limits on the subject. There is no need to turn into a complete killjoy on the quest for consistency. Follow your instincts. They're hardly ever wrong. The important thing here is that you paint your railings with bright colors, so your child doesn't miss them.

Remain as calm as you can. When establishing house rules, a no-nonsense demeanor tells the child that your words should be taken seriously. Be stern but kind. Each time you remain calm, you keep the spotlight not on the toddler but on the behavior. This is probably easier in theory, right? It is a huge challenge trying to manage your temper when your 2 years old just pushed a full crate of eggs off the shelf, or when your one year old drops your phone in a bowl of water, or when your three years old mistakenly dumps the contents of your makeup box into the toilet. The only thing on your mind in any of these scenarios would be "Hell no!" which is quite understandable. However, yelling is not going to gain you any points because it is highly degrading and fruitless.

When you raise your voice, you are emitting very strong negative emotions that you don't want your impressionable toddler to pick up. The only thing yelling might accomplish to make you feel somewhat better because you just expressed an emotion instead of bottling it up — plus, there's a good chance you just inspired your child to scream at others later. Your reaction will have a much stronger and lasting effect if it is delivered rationally and calmly. If all you feel at that moment is fury, then take a few seconds to relax enough to intervene. Some people count to ten or do some Lamaze breathing to calm their nerves.

A reaction that is too lenient is just as effective as yelling. If your child can sense a hint of uncertainty or mildness in your response, consider that message diluted. As much as you can, steer clear of reactions that seem like questions. Example, "Stop drawing on the wall, okay, baby?" Would you like to go to bed right now?" and so on. On the other hand, make attempts not to give instruction while you're laughing. It is understandably difficult to maintain a stern look when your toddler is completely wrapped in toilet paper. You have two options in situations like this: You can choose to laugh and let it go or issue a correction while looking as stern as you can at that moment. You can go laugh in private when you're done. Laughter sends a confusing message. It's like telling your child that you're serious but not quite, and this is impractical. If you decide you want to intervene rather than let it go, do so with the right amount of firmness.

Keep it as brief as possible. When trying to get your message across to your toddler, use as few words as you can. There is absolutely no need to stray into, for example, medical facts about why stuffing dried corn up a person's nose is not good. Your toddler will benefit more from short and direct messages like, "We don't do that." "Don't run, walk." "Hitting hurts." "Not safe." etc.

Also, consider your child's temperament when dishing out discipline. A one size fits all mentality will not do much for you in toddler discipline. Some toddlers are easygoing and react positively to gentle reminders and one warning. Other toddlers have more demanding and intense personalities. These might need more firmness and strict limits. If you happen to give in once to toddlers like this, they are likely to take advantage of it and repeat the behavior. Try to remain open-minded to discover better approaches that might work for you and your child. Your child's temperament shines forth brighter than ever during toddlerhood, and it is at this time where you will get to discover your child and what works for the family.

Stop expecting miracles. Discipline is a gradual process. Turning an untamed toddler into a well-mannered citizen will take a lot of years. It goes way past toddlerhood and the teen years. Total discipline will not happen overnight, so you have to learn to be patient. At some point, you'll notice you have been saying the same thing over and over and wondering why the child still repeats the behavior. Lessons like "Say please," and "Stop running. Walk" tend to be put on repeat, and it can be the most frustrating thing. I have a few friends who normally don't like repeating themselves, so I know.

I suggest you construct the most used reminders using the exact words every time you say them. For example, "If you hit, you sit," "Pee on the floor, clean up more. Pee in a line, everything is fine." I know sometimes, it seems like the lessons you put on repeat have no effect at all, but that's not true. The effect is progressive, and one day your toddler won't need to hear you say it anymore. They are constantly absorbing information even when they are clearly in defiance or look to be in ignorance. One day he won't need you to tell him to pee directly into the bowl without getting it all over the floor.

Don't forget always to set a good example. I've seen parents hit their children as a disciplinary measure for hitting. You don't slap your toddler's hand while saying, "We don't hit." That is counterintuitive, and silly because you just hit. Parents also do a lot of grabbing. This is a negative response or form of expression. It is more respectful to calmly ask the child to give it to you in a matter of fact tone. Hold out your hand for emphasis or softly uncurl her fingers from around whatever it is, and say something along the lines of "not safe." It is good to do as you preach because toddlers are more interested in imitating actions than listening to corrective words.

Having a child is the best thing that can happen to anyone. Parenthood is almost like starting life afresh, and it is just as exciting as it is scary knowing that you created your own human and are responsible for it. You get to grow while your child grows and learn while your child learns. No parent knows it all, not even me. It won't all be all sunshine and rainbows, but one day you will look back on the days when your child was just three years old, innocent and free of worries, and realize that you wouldn't trade those moments for anything in the world. As a parent, you have to be open to correction and new means to make life easier for you and your baby. Whatever happens, just remember that it is a journey where you and your toddler discover yourself and each other. For them, everything is worth it.

References

1, 2, 3…The Toddler Years, Irene Van der Zande. Published by Santa Cruz Toddler Care Center (1986)

Claire Lerner, LCSW-C, child development specialist; director of parenting resources, Zero to Three.

Dear Parent: Caring for Infants with Respect, Magda Gerber. Published by Resources for Infant Educarers (2002)

How To Talk So Kids Will Listen & Listen So Kids Will Talk, Adele Faber & Elaine Mazlish, Published by Avon Books (1980)

Infants, Toddlers, and Caregivers, Janet Gonzalez-Mena, Dianne Widmeyer Eyer. Published by Mayfield Publishing Company (1997)

Lisa Asta, MD, pediatrician, Walnut Creek, Calif.; associate clinical professor of pediatrics, University of California, San Francisco.

No-Drama Discipline, Daniel J. Siegel, M.D. & Tina Payne Bryson, PhD. Published by Bantam (2014)

Raising Your Spirited Child, Mary Sheedy Kurcinka, Published by HarperCollins (2012)

Say What You See For Parents and Teachers, Sandra R. Blackard. Published by Language of Listening (2012)

Siblings Without Rivalry, Adele Faber & Elaine Mazlish. Published by W.W. Norton & Co (2012)

Straus M.A. Archives of Pediatric Adolescent Medicine, 1997.

The Emotional Life of the Toddler, Alicia F. Lieberman, Ph.D.. Published by The Free Press (1995)

Your Self-Confident Baby, Magda Gerber, Allison Johnson. Published by John Wiley & Sons, Inc. (1998)